★ ★ ★ ★ ★

BORN TO REIGN

★ ★ ★ ★ ★

JOSEPH AGUNBIADE

DEDICATION

★ ★ ★ ★ ★

I dedicate this book to my children and everyone who desires to fulfil their glorious destiny.

You are born to Reign

You are destined for greatness

You are destined for significance

ACKNOWLEDGMENTS

✯ ✯ ✯ ✯ ✯

I thank God Almighty for granting me the grace to write this book. To Him be all the glory and honour.

I acknowledge the support, encouragements and immense contributions of my wife, Adeolu. She is a priceless asset to my life, family and ministry. Thank you so much my darling for your partnership and for co-labouring with me.

I acknowledge my parents and my parents-in- law. I appreciate their love and contributions to my life.

I also acknowledge the contributions of my spiritual parents, Bishop Mike Bamidele and Reverend (Mrs) Titi Bamidele. I appreciate their love, wise counsels, prayers and oversight over my life and ministry.

Special thanks also to Stephanie Leger and Sheryl Mkwananzi. I appreciate the time and efforts you put to proofread the manuscript. I am also indebted to Ekaete Inyang who edited the manuscript. You are stars!

I would like to thank Nigel and Tracy Seaborne for their prayers and encouragement. Your encouragement helped me to push on.

Finally, I thank my children, Emmanuel, Joshua & Joseph (Jr) for their encouragements, support and understanding while I was writing this book.

TABLE OF CONTENTS

☆ ☆ ☆ ☆ ☆

BORN TO REIGN

FOREWORD

I first conceived the idea for this book in January 2012 while conducting a naming and child dedication service in our church.

Before I started writing I was clear about my goal and objective: to write a faith building, motivational book that will inspire, encourage and challenge anyone who reads it to a greater sense of awareness of their purpose, potential and tremendous possibilities ahead of them. Having this goal in mind, I prayerfully and purposefully selected the subject matter of each chapter. This took me several months to conclude.

As an angel on assignment, I am fully convinced that this book will encourage, inspire and challenge you to move further, deeper and faster in the direction of your destiny, purpose or mission no matter your challenges, limitations and setbacks.

One of the moments I look forward to when I play Monopoly is when I get a community chess or chance card that provides me with the opportunity to either get out of jail free or advance to go. These opportunities usually come at critical moments in the game when I feel helpless, trapped or unsure of how to turn the game around to my advantage. In the same way, I pray that this book will be to you like a community chess or chance card for the issues you may be facing right now.

I am confident that as you read this book, you will receive timely insights, inspirations, encouragements, guidance, wisdom, understanding and boldness that will empower you to break free from any limitation, bondage or mediocrity and advance to your glorious and wealthy place.

I pray that the God of all hope and grace empower you with His grace, love and favour in Jesus name.

Joseph Agunbiade

CHAPTER ONE

DESTINED TO REIGN

A long time ago there lived a young woman in a small town. She fell in love with a carpenter. They got engaged and planned to marry as soon as possible. The woman became pregnant with a miracle baby. In those days the emperor of their state made a decree that a census should be carried out. Everyone had to go to their hometown to be registered. It took the couple a long time to get back to their hometown as they did not have cars or any other fast means of transport back in those days. When they reached their hometown, all the hotels and lodges for travellers were full and there was nowhere for them to stay. They managed to find a small barn where animals were kept to stay for the night. That night an exciting and wonderful thing happened. The woman went into labour and gave birth to a baby boy. But he wasn't just any baby. He was destined to save the world. He was named Jesus.

Jesus was not born in a fancy palace or even in a hospital. He was born in a manger. Nevertheless, He was destined to reign. He was destined for greatness. He was born to reign. I don't know the circumstances into which you were born. One thing I know is that God has destined you for greatness. You are destined to reign. You are born for significance. You are born to be celebrated.

Melanie Amaro was born in Fort Lauderdale, Florida but was raised in Tortola, British Virgin Islands from the age of three. Melanie was sent to the British Virgin Island to live with her grandmother after her parents felt they did not have the means to provide for her. While Melanie's mother was pregnant, a man of God told her that the child she was carrying had a song. Nineteen years later, Melanie won the first season of The X Factor USA in December 2011, securing a $5 million recording contract with Syco music and Epic records. Walking through the doors of opportunity, Melanie will do what she was born to do: sing. She was born to reign. She was destined for greatness!

Doors of Opportunity

Although you may not be aware, there are doors of opportunity waiting for you! According to the Bible in Revelation 3: 8 God says

"I know thy works: behold, I have set before thee an open door, and no man can shut it: for thou has a little strength, and has kept my word, and has not denied my name."

The phrase "I know thy works" also refers to your diligence, practice, efforts, discipline and persistence. God rewards our efforts. He brings opportunities. You may not know when your door of opportunity is going to open. It may come early in your life or later, but your door will open someday. In the meantime, you must get ready, sharpen your skills, practice, train, study, pray and be proactive.

The Bible records the story of a young boy called David. He was still a teenager, probably between 15 to 17 years old, when his door of opportunity opened. His father sent him on an errand to carry food provisions to his older brothers who were at the battle line, defending their nation, Israel. While there, David heard Goliath, a champion out of the camp of the Philistines, shouting his daily defiance at the armies of Israel. He saw how the giant stirred great fear within the men of Israel. He volunteered to fight Goliath and managed to persuade King Saul to allow him to fight the giant. Although David hadn't been on the battle line before, he was prepared. How, you might ask? He had practised; he sharpened his skill in using a catapult. He had faced lions and bears. He had confronted personal problems which developed his faith and trust in God. He boldly responded to King Saul's concerns that he was a youth.

The Bible records David's response to the King in 1 Samuel 17: 34-37 (NIV).

"But David said to Saul, "Your servant has been keeping his father's sheep. When a lion or a bear came and carried off a sheep from the flock, I went after it, struck it, and rescued the sheep from its mouth. When it turned on me, I seized it by its hair, struck it and killed it. Your servant has killed both the lion and the bear; this uncircumcised Philistine will be like one of them, because he has defied the armies of the living God. The LORD who rescued me from the paw of the lion and the paw of the bear will rescue me from the hand of this Philistine."

Saul said to David, "Go, and the Lord be with you."

David was proactive. The door of opportunity opened for him to be noticed by the King. In Proverbs 22:29, the Bible states that "a man diligent in his works will stand before kings."

Even when it appears that you have exhausted all of your resources, when there seems to be no way out or you feel you cannot take another step, God is still able to make a way for you. He still has doors of opportunity to open for you. I love the comforting and assuring song by Don Moen: *God will make a way.* Yes, He will surely make a way for you. He works in ways that the human mind cannot comprehend. His ways are higher, better and more rewarding than human ways.

Do you feel you're in a dead end situation right now? It appears there is no other way, no one to turn to for help and you cannot see any way out? Fear not, God will make a way for you. He has made ways for millions of people in every generation. He will surely make a way for you too. He will open doors of opportunity beyond your imaginations. God is not limited in where, how and when he can open your door of opportunity. He is omnipresent. He has the master key and master plan. He can open the door any time, in any place, and even in the most obscure situations.

Despite Joseph being in prison, God opened his door of opportunity whilst he was incarcerated. God gave Pharaoh, the king of Egypt, a dream that he didn't understand and therefore had to be interpreted. No one could interpret the dream except Joseph. It was Joseph's time. The King's dream was Joseph's door of opportunity to significance. He walked out of prison to palace. He moved from prison to praise, from limitation to freedom, from obscurity to significance!

Someone somewhere has a question that only you can answer, a problem that probably only you can solve, tears that only you can wipe away. Someone has a fear that only you can remove, a weakness that only you can strengthen, a wound that only you can heal, pain that only you can relieve. Someone out there has a dream that only you can interpret, a vision that only you can fulfil and a gap that only you can fill. When you recognise the needs around you and help people solve their problems, you are moving closer to your door of opportunity. You are closer to fulfilling your own dreams.

You are closer than you think

You may not know it, but God is working in the background like a coach and is moving you in the direction of your dream. You are born to reign. You are destined for significance. God is about to move you from obscurity to significance. It may not feel like it but you are closer than you think.

Think about it. Leona Lewis probably didn't realise she was close to her dream of becoming a singer and songwriter when she was working as a receptionist at a mortgage broker. Like many other hopefuls in the UK, Leona lined up for a chance to showcase her talent and be recognised worldwide through The X Factor. Leona had cultivated her talent since she was very young. Her parents enrolled her into Sylvie Young Theatre School when she was only five. She attended the Brit School for Performing Arts & Technology, where she learned to play musical instruments, such as the guitar and piano, in the hopes of becoming a singer-songwriter. Leona tried her best to get a recording deal, but never managed to get a contract. She took a variety of jobs, including working as a waitress and receptionist to earn money to pay for time in a recording studio. She nearly gave up; and who would have blamed her? She must have thought 'this is never going to happen for me'.

Leona auditioned for The X Factor in 2006. She consistently won praises from all three judges on the show. It was clear that Leona was the dominant contestant in the competition and she won the finals easily with about sixty percent of the votes. The prize; a one million pound recording contract plus the priceless opportunity to spread her wings and fly.

I was among the millions of fans watching her live on the 20th December 2006 as she sang her final song *A Moment Like This*. I was moved by her tears and excitement as she struggled to accept the reality that her dream had finally come true. *A Moment Like This* was downloaded a staggering 50,000 times in the 30 minutes after The X Factor competition. Selling over half a million copies in its first week, the song continued to sell over the rest of the week after the competition. Today, Leona Lewis is a multi-platinum selling artist and three time Grammy Award nominee. She has sold over 20 million records worldwide, making her the most successful artist in history to come from a reality TV show. She was born to reign. She was born for significance.

Like Leona, your moment of opportunity is coming. You are closer than you think. Maybe all you need is one more application or one more phone call. Perhaps the next interview will be the one that has a positive outcome, or you just need a bit more practice, to do a few more lessons, more research, and give that extra push.

I was in the labour room with my wife when she was about to deliver our second child, Joshua. She had been experiencing contractions early, for over a week before he was born. I had already taken her to the hospital twice that week only to be asked to go back home. Two days before the delivery date, she was having intermittent contractions. I had to rush her to the hospital again. In the labour ward the pain was becoming almost unbearable despite having been given an epidural. That night as she held my hand, I was praying gently for God to take perfect control. She was focused on the pain, while the midwife was measuring her cervical dilation. Each moment her cervix was expanding, preparing an easy passage for the coming baby. Indeed she was closer than she thought! With encouragement and persistence, despite the unceasing pain she gave another push, another push and yet another push. I saw the baby's head and body coming out as the midwife helped pull the baby out. Within seconds the baby was out. I quickly cuddled my wife. What a relief and joy my wife and I had that night, looking at our new-born child! The news had quickly gone round the family and everyone called to rejoice with us!

The Bible records in Luke 1:57-58 (NIV) *"When it was time for Elizabeth to have her baby, she gave birth to a son. Her neighbours and relatives heard that the Lord had shown her great mercy, and they shared her joy."*

Your own moment of joy is fast approaching. When your moment comes, you forget the pain, discomfort, sleepless nights, solitudes, disappointments, rejections, misunderstandings, inadequacies, insufficiencies, and even failures. You are closer than you think.

In Psalm 40:3 (NIV), the Psalmist writes

*"He put a new song in my mouth,
a hymn of praise to our God.
Many will see and fear the LORD
and put their trust in him."*

Relax, and take on each new day with thanksgiving as you trust God to bring your moment of opportunity and fulfilment. When you cultivate an attitude of thanksgiving and appreciate God for your present circumstances, the songs will not just be in your mouth, they will be stored in your heart.

Mary who was to be the mother of Jesus understood the importance of praising and appreciating God even when the promise had not yet fully manifested. She knew how to hold on to the promise and encourage and rejoice with others, even when she was at risk of being misunderstood and labelled unfaithful by those who did not understand she was carrying a heavenly impacted vision. The Bible records how she expressed her appreciation to God in Luke 1:46-55 when the angel of God told her she would be pregnant with a miracle child.

"And Mary said:
'My soul glorifies the Lord
and my spirit rejoices in God my Saviour,
for he has been mindful
of the humble state of his servant.
From now on all generations will call me blessed,
for the Mighty One has done great things for me—
holy is his name.
His mercy extends to those who fear him,
from generation to generation.
He has performed mighty deed]s with his arm;
he has scattered those who are proud in their inmost
     thoughts.
He has brought down rulers from their thrones
but has lifted up the humble.
He has filled the hungry with good things
but has sent the rich away empty.
He has helped his servant Israel,
remembering to be merciful
to Abraham and his descendants forever,
just as he promised our ancestors.'" (NIV)

God is about to do great things for you. He is about to bless you beyond your imagination. He is about to replace your struggles with favour. He is about to release new things into your life and circumstances. He is bringing new opportunities, new relationships, new inspirations, new revelations, new understandings and new strategies.

Arise & Shine

At the moment you may look insignificant and unimportant in the eyes of people around you. You may even feel insignificant. Surely you are born to reign. As a child of God, you are a prince or princess. You are joint heir with Christ Jesus to the throne.

In 1 John 3:1-2 (NIV), the Bible states as follows:

"See what great love the Father has lavished on us, that we should be called children of God! And that is what we are! The reason the world does not know us is that it did not know him. Dear friends, now we are children of God, and what we will be has not yet been made known. But we know that when Christ appears, we shall be like him, for we shall see him as he is."

As a young boy, I enjoyed watching films, especially comedy, and still watch films occasionally, despite my busy schedule. One of the films I found interesting in those days was "Coming to America", starring Eddie Murphy, who plays an African prince.

In the film, Akeem Joffer (Eddie Murphy) is a prince and heir to the throne of a fictitious wealthy African country called Zamunda. He is discontented with being pampered all his life and travels to America with the hope of finding a woman who he can both love and respect and who will accept him for who he is, not because of status.

Akeem and his personal aide arrive in Queens, New York City. They rent a rundown apartment in Jamaica, one of the neighbourhoods, pretending to be poor foreign students and managed to get a job at a local fast food restaurant called McDowells. Akeem falls in love with Lisa, daughter of Cleo McDowell, who is the owner of the restaurant. Although Akeem thrives on working hard and seeing how commoners live, his personal aide (Semni) is not comfortable with the life of a poor man in America and has to plead for financial help from Akeem's parents in Africa.

The royal couple (Akeem's parents) decide to travel to United States and reveal themselves to the McDowells. The McDowells are surprised when the true identity of Akeem is revealed: a prince! An heir to the throne of a powerful and wealthy king!

Do you recognise that you are a prince or princess? You are an heir or heiress to a great and awesome heritage. Your natural parents may not be as rich or as powerful as Akeem's parents, but you have a heavenly Father. He owns the heavens and the earth. He is the King of Kings and the Lord of Lords.

For now you may not look like a prince or princess. You may even be living in a run-down, rat infested apartment. Maybe you cannot even afford a flat of your own and have found yourself sharing with friends and family. You may even be struggling to afford a decent meal. You may be working at a job that is not befitting; overlooked for promotions and pay rises. Or you may be unemployed and wondering if it will ever get better. The time is coming when your identity as a child of God will be revealed. You are born to reign. You are born for significance.

The Bible states that when Jesus was born, he was brought to the temple by his parents on the seventh day to be dedicated to the Lord. A man of God whose name was Simeon also came to the temple to worship. When he saw Jesus, he praised God and said to Mary that the child she had was set for the rising of many in Israel. As a prophet of God, I am declaring to you through this message that you have been selected to be among the people that God is raising up. You are part of the special people God is moving from obscurity to significance. You are a seed of greatness planted by God ripe for harvest. Arise; shine; for your light has come. The glory of God is rising upon you!

CHAPTER TWO

UNDERSTAND YOUR VALUE

Venus Williams – widely known as one of the greatest female tennis players of all time – has shown the world how far drive, confidence, and a winning spirit could take her. She has reigned as world No 1 women tennis player on three separate occasions and was credited as ushering a new, modern power and athletism on women's professional tennis. The four-time Olympic gold medallist and multiple Grand Slam tennis champion once said. "You have to believe in yourself when no one does – that makes you a winner right there."

Your self-worth is very important. It has to come from within. You are valuable and have great talents and abilities (Chapter 4 on "Maximising your potential" will deal with this in more detail).

Beyonce, an American singer, actress and former member of R&B girls' group Destiny's Child, said. "Your self-worth is determined by you. You don't have to depend on someone telling you who you are." And she's right. If you depend wholly on people telling you who you are, or who you are supposed to be, someone will eventually tell you who you are not.

Although Jesus walked on earth as a man, He had a positive image about Himself and His assignment. He would not allow men to place their own value on Him. He knew He was a King, Saviour and Redeemer. He was not bragging around about His deity but He certainly understood the value that God placed on Him. He talked and acted based on His understanding of His value and mission. When asked, He said to people: *"I am the resurrection and the life"; "I am the way, the truth and the life"; "I am the bread of life"; and "I am the good Shepherd."*

Your value is not based on someone's inability to see your worth

The dictionary defines self-worth as "the opinion you have about yourself and the value you place on yourself." Your self-worth is your ability to appreciate your own value and accept yourself, independent of other people's opinion. Of course, we all want to feel loved, appreciated and accepted by others, however, you have to be whole and complete in yourself. No one else can do that for you. Your value is not based on someone's inability to see your worth. People are usually impatient and may not tolerate your little beginnings. Don't despise your own little beginnings.

Walt Disney, the pioneer of motion picture film and creator of Disneyland and Micky Mouse, was at one time fired by a newspaper editor because he felt "he lacked imagination and had no good ideas".

How ironic! The rejected went on to create one of the largest entertainment industries using creativity and imagination. Walt Disney became a major figure within the American animation industry and was well known throughout the world for his influence and contribution to the field of entertainment during the 20th Century. In his lifetime he received four honorary Academy awards, won seven Emmy Awards, and gave his name to Walt Disney World resort theme parks not only in the United States, but also international resorts in

Tokyo, Paris and Hong Kong. You have probably heard of the Walt Disney World Resort in Florida? Maybe you've visited or are wishing to visit with your family? Did you know that it is the most visited attraction in the world, with yearly record attendance of 52.5 million people! The resort was designed and planned by Walt Disney before he died in 1966. Although Disney World Resort was built after his death, the resort was named in honour of his name and legacy.

Oprah Winfrey was also fired from her former job as a junior reporter. The producer told her she "was not fit for television." Oprah is now a media proprietor, talk show host, actress, producer and philanthropist. She is best known for her multi-award winning talk show 'The Oprah Winfrey Show" that aired nationally in America for 25 seasons. The show received 47 Daytime Emmy Awards before it ended in May 2011 and remains the highest rated talk show in American television history.

The first African American Academy Award winner for Best Actor, Sidney Poitier, was told after his first audition by the casting director, "Why don't you stop wasting people's time and go out and become a dishwasher or something?" It was at that moment, recalls Poitier that he decided to devote his life to acting. He went on to win the Academy Award for Best Actor for his role in *"Lilies of the Field"* in 1964. In 1967, he starred in the *"In the Heat of The Night"* and *"Guess Who's Coming To Dinner"*, making him the top box-office star of that year. In 1999, he was named among the Greatest Male Stars of All Time by American Film Institute. In 2009, he was awarded the Presidential Medal of Freedom, the United States of America's highest civilian honour, by President Barack Obama.

In your journey, you may find yourself in need of help or assistance. Whatever the situation, you should not allow people to undermine your value. In 1 Samuel 25, the Bible records that David was on the run from King Saul who was trying to kill him. While in the wilderness, David asked a wealthy man named Nabal for food for his men and himself. Although David had reached out to Nabal with a blessing of goodwill, Nabal shows nothing but contempt for David and his men. Apparently, Nabal did not know that David was destined to reign. David would soon be a king. David was not a weak man of no account. He was a great soldier and warrior.

God does not see you as weak; in His eyes, you are a mighty man or woman of strength. God is looking at your potential. He is looking at the strength, gifts, talents and abilities that He has put in you, which men may disregard or neglect. In Judges 6:14, the Bible records that God said to Gideon *"Go in the strength you have and save Israel out of the Midian's hand"* (NIV). God is not focusing on your weaknesses, He is focusing on your potential. Men may focus on your weaknesses but not God. I encourage you to also focus on your strengths and potential rather than your weaknesses. Do not undervalue yourself. You are worth much more than people may think or say about you.

You may be working in a low-valued job, receiving a low salary and appear insignificant in the eyes of people around you. Nevertheless, your true value is not based on your current job, your house, or the type of car you drive. Your true value is based on your purpose and the contribution you are already making, or are destined to make on earth. The Bible records in the third chapter of Esther that the entire King's servants were bowing down to a man by the name Haman. But Mordecai, a gatekeeper refused to bow to him. Why? He understood his value was not based on where he stays 24hrs of the day - at the King's gate. His true value and worth was based on saving the life of the King by exposing the two chamberlains who had conspired to kill him. His true value was recognised when the King honoured him with the royal robe the King had worn, the royal horse the King had ridden and the royal crown the King had worn. Your true value is about recognising and being rewarded with favour and honour.

In life there will always be someone who will try to undermine or bring you down. That is part of life experience, but you have to stay positive about yourself. Do not allow negative words and negative opinion of naysayers and critics make you doubt yourself and your God-given abilities. I love the way David responded to his brother Eliab when he spoke negatively to him, trying to discourage him from taking up the challenge of Goliath.

The Bible records in 1 Samuel 17:28 that when Eliab, David's oldest brother, heard him speaking with the other men in the battlefield, he burned with anger at him and asked, *"Why have you come down here? And with whom did you leave those few sheep in the wilderness? I know how conceited you are and how wicked your heart is; you came down only to watch the battle"* (NIV).

However, David simply responded by saying *"Now what have I done. Can't I even speak?" He then turned away to someone else and brought up the same matter, and the men answered him as before.* Amazing! David did not engage in much conversation with his brother, he simply moved away from him and walked towards someone else who would grant him audience. David's attitude was, "I know my value. You cannot define or determine my worth. God has placed greater value and worth on me than you can imagine. That's why He rescued me from the lion and the bear, and He has given me the ability to overcome this uncircumcised Philistine. I will not tolerate your negative words. I will not allow you to distract me. This is my moment of opportunity. You wait and see what the Lord will do through me!"

We've all probably been there, feeling victimised by a family member, friend, elder, colleague, employer, boss, competitor, or any other person who has treated us unfairly.

I remember a personal experience when I was working as a junior lawyer in one of the reputable law firms in Nigeria. I was in the High Court one day representing one of our clients in a land dispute case. The Defence Counsel was a senior lawyer designated Senior Advocate of Nigeria (SAN), the equivalent of the Queen's Counsel in UK. My boss was also a Senior Advocate but was indisposed and unable to attend court sittings that day. She had instructed me during our case briefing to cross-examine two of the defence witnesses. However, the defence team were not willing to proceed with their case. They were seeking for an adjournment; actually three consecutive adjournments at each court sitting. I stood up to object to another motion for adjournment by the Defence Counsel. As soon as I raised the objection, the Defence Counsel raised his voice at me saying "Sit down, you are a junior". However, I refused to be intimidated by him and continued stating my reasons for opposing the motion. Thank God, the Judge and other lawyers in the courtroom, both seniors and juniors, reacted to the remarks of the senior counsel. He had to apologise for his unprofessional remarks.

Do you realise that your energy, confidence, attitude and body language are the currency that others will transact with? You may not know, but you allow people to treat you the way they do. I've learned to embrace positive self-worth. I am still a student in this journey; however, I am determined not to allow anyone to put their price tag on me. I am sure you will also not want anyone to put their price tag on you. No, never! You are worth more than Gold.

I read a story about an experiment in a psychology class. The tutor puts labels on the foreheads of all the students. Everyone else could see the label on each student except the owner of the label. At the start of the group discussion, the tutor instructed the students to treat each other according to the label. One girl was labelled "insignificant" and the group treated her according to the label on her forehead. No one asked her anything. They skipped past her as if she wasn't there. When she said something or tried to contribute to the discussion, everyone ignored her. Eventually she stopped trying to be part of the discussion and just sat looking sad and angry. People will treat you according to how you portray yourself. Although you have no label on your head, but how you feel about yourself shows in how you talk, what you say about yourself, the look on your face, and many other things.

Focus on the positive attributes about you. Look at what you can do. Do not worry too much on what you cannot do. If you worry too much on what you cannot do, it will rob you of those things you can do. If you focus on what you can do, other people will come your way that will help you do what you cannot do. There are many people who cannot do what you can do. They will seek your help too. They desperately need what you can do.

In Judges 11, the Bible tells the story of an outcast Jephthah, who was berated and forced out of town by his half-brothers because he was born out of wedlock.

His mother was a prostitute. However, God had great plans for him. Despite his humiliation and exile, he rose above his circumstances. He gained experience as a warrior and a group of young men joined him and he became known as a mighty warrior. Sometime later, the Ammonites invaded his nation Israel. The elders of Israel had to look for him and begged him to come home and lead their army against the enemies. He was their only hope for victory. He agreed, but with a condition that if he is successful, they must vow to accept him as their leader. They had no choice. They were desperate for help and so agreed to his requests. He became captain over Israel's army and God gave him great victory over the Ammonites. He became an influential judge in the whole of Israel. He gained the respect of his brothers and family who initially rejected him.

I am convinced that Jephthah developed a sense of positive self-worth despite his negative background. He did not allow the rejection by his brothers to determine his life. God is aware of your past. He is in your present and has great plans for you. Do not allow your negative background to hinder your destiny. You can rise above your past circumstances and limitations. Yes, you can rise above your discouragements and doubts; surely you can rise above rejections. God will not give up on you. Don't you dare give up on yourself.

You are Valued by God

You were created in the image of God, your maker. The Bible reveals in Psalm 8 that God has crowned you with glory and honour. Yes he did! You are beautifully and wonderfully made by God. Your self-worth should be based on the value placed on you by God and not on the opinion of people. The value that God placed on you is constant, despite your imperfection, weaknesses or failures. By the way, all men have weaknesses, even the greatest of men. God values you based on His character and not based on your perfection or weakness. God will not despise you, reject you or undermine you because of your weakness. Rather, He will comfort, uphold and strengthen you. Even when you fail or make mistakes, God will not undermine you. He still believes in you. He constantly sees the treasures, potential and greatness in you and He wants you to see it too. Our Creator has made each of us unique and distinct from each other. There is no one exactly like you and never will be. Whoa! You are here on earth for a distinctive purpose.

You may be going through a situation in your life that you may feel like nobody cares, but be rest assured your Heavenly Father cares about you. He will provide for your needs, He will preserve you and He will help you. The Bible records in Luke 12:6-7, that Jesus encouraged his disciples in saying that since God cares about the well-being of sparrows, they should be rest assured that God will take care of their needs.

Sparrows are some of most common birds in the world. They are small, plump, brown-grey birds with short tails and powerful beaks. They are one of the smallest of all birds in the animal kingdom, yet the Bible tells us that not one of them is forgotten by God. In the eyes of man, these birds are not worth much. In Jesus' time, two sparrows were sold for a farthing (less than one cent), but to God, they have great value. Not even one sparrow dies or falls to the ground unnoticed by God. If God cares so much about the well-being of the sparrows, then how much more does God care about you? You are definitely of much value than sparrows. He cares so much about you. You have great value and significance in the eyes of God. Friend, I encourage you to put on the contact lenses of God and see yourself the way God does.

In 2 Samuel Chapter 9, the Bible records how King David showed kindness to Mephibosheth, King Saul's grandson. His father, Jonathan, was a close covenant friend to David before his tragic death in the battle against the Philistines. King Saul was also killed in the battle. When the news of the King and Jonathan's death reached the palace, Mephibosheth's nurse panicked. She quickly carried the five year old boy and tried to flee to safety in case the enemies invaded the palace. Somehow, she lost her grip and dropped Mephibosheth. The fall was very severe and he was crippled for life.

Now because he was crippled, Mephibosheth had a poor self-image. Instead of seeing himself as the rightful heir to his father's and grandfather's legacy, he saw himself as a dead dog. However, when David became King, he recalled the family of Jonathan, his former best friend, and discovered that Mephibosheth was still alive. He sent royal messengers to bring Mephibostheth to the palace. When Mephibosheth was brought to the palace, King David told him that he intended to show him kindness. The King blessed him and restored his lost inheritance.

Can you relate to the story of Mephibosheth? Maybe someone dropped you sometime in your life knowingly or unknowingly, wilfully or unintentionally, carelessly or innocently and the experience has turned your whole world upside down. It could be your parents, spouse, close relative, friend, or employer. Maybe your father or mother abandoned you, or denied you of parental love and approval that could have helped you grow up in life. Maybe you were dropped by your spouse and the trauma and pain of rejection or divorce has left you crippled, spiritually, emotionally, mentally, financially, psychologically and socially. You feel you're alone, robbed of your sense of dignity and self-worth. God can pick you up just as King David showed kindness and restored the lost inheritance, honour and dignity to Mephibosheth. He can restore your honour and dignity and make you a beacon of light and hope to others.

Late Archbishop Benson Idahosa was a charismatic Pentecostal preacher and founder of Church of God Mission International, with headquarters in Nigeria. He was renowned for his robust faith and often referred to as father of Pentecostalism in Nigeria. His childhood story was remarkable. He was born to non-Christian parents in a predominantly non-Christian community. He was rejected by his father for being frail and sickly. He constantly had fainting spells and on one of those spells his mother abandoned him at a rubbish heap presuming him dead. Hours later he began wailing and was later picked up by his mother. He grew up in a poor household and denied education until he was fourteen years old. However, God had great plans for his life.

He got converted to Christianity as a youth and became zealous in winning souls and in conducting evangelistic outreaches in villages in the eastern part of Nigeria where he was brought up. His faith in God and understanding of the value placed on him by God helped him develop self-confidence and positive attitude to life. He was known for his boldness, power and prosperity-based preaching, as well as enormous faith in the supernatural. He was known for many notable quotes including "Your attitude determines your altitude"; "I am a possibilitarian"; and "If your faith says yes, God cannot say no". He ministered in over 143 countries all over the world and is reported to have performed so many remarkable miracles, including healing of the blind and even raising the dead. As at the time of his death in 1998, he had preached in over 145 nations.

A lot of people are painfully conscious of their weaknesses and things that hold them back but are unable to see their strengths, abilities, talents and uniqueness. They focus on their weaknesses to the detriment of their strengths and capabilities. They are constantly discouraged, depressed, and feel intimidated and inferior to others.

Your self-worth is based on the value you place on yourself and what you think about yourself. In the writings of Apostle Paul recorded in Philippians chapter 4 verse 8, he encourages believers to "think on what is true, noble, right, pure, lovely, admirable, excellent and praiseworthy." Are you constantly thinking of noble and admirable things about yourself? Or do you constantly settle for less than you deserve or make someone your priority while you are just their option?

Friend, don't settle for less. Only the best is good for you. You are God's best creation! You are God's most adored creation.

Joel Osteen, Pastor of Lakewood, a mega church in Houston, Texas, tells a story in his bestselling book, "*Your best life now*". Years ago, Joel Osteen's dad, the founding pastor of the Church, went to a high school football game with his friend Jesse. They were especially interested in watching the performance of Jesse's son Jeff, who was a defence player. Playing on defence, Jeff rarely got an opportunity to touch the football. But on one particular play when the other team was in the punt formation, the punter kicked a short punt. Jeff ran over, caught the ball, took a half step to his right and a half step back to his left, his eyes darting in every direction, searching for some daylight. But there was no running room to be found. Just then, about ten guys from the opposing team clobbered him. Consequently, he didn't advance the ball one inch. For a long awkward moment Joel Osteen's dad sat silently staring out at the field, feeling bad for Jesse and trying to think of something good to say as the play had been a disaster for Jeff's team. Joel's dad, however, could not come up with anything positive to say about the match. While he was still pondering about the match, Jesse came up to him and punched him in the ribs with a big smile on his face saying "Pastor, did you see those two good moves?" Joel Osteen concluded that "Only a loving father could see his son's two good moves and that's exactly how God sees us. He is not dwelling on the time we get knocked down; he is not dwelling on our faults. He sees our two good moves."

You may not be aware, but God sees your two good moves. Even one good move is significant in the eyes of God. Many times we allow our failures, weaknesses and fear to take centre stage. We allow the critical words, threats, intimidations and harassments from people to make us feel discouraged, depressed, inferior and worthless. We dwell on those and quickly forget about the two good moves we have made. God doesn't. He knows you have more moves in you. He can see a potential dozen moves you can make towards fulfilment of your God-given destiny.

After a 3 year drought in Samaria, Elijah presented himself to King Ahab with the promise that God would provide rain. He then challenged the 450 prophets of Baal to a contest on a Mountain called Camel to prove the supremacy of God over Baal and idol worship. Baal was a god of the Canaanites that was worshipped even by the people of God. Elijah challenged the prophets of Baal to set up a sacrificial alter and call on Baal to set it alight. But nothing happened. Elijah likewise set up an altar, doused his sacrifice with water - filling a trench around the altar - and called on God to light his sacrifice. God answered his prayers and sent down fire and burnt up the sacrifice, the wood, stones and dried up the water in the trench. When the people saw the clear victory of God over Baal, they fell on their faces and said "The Lord, He is God". Elijah then ordered the people to kill all the prophets of Baal as they were false prophets. After the execution of the false prophets Elijah prayed for rain to end the three year drought in Israel. God produced a torrential downpour in answer to Elijah's prayer. However, Jezebel, the wife of King Ahab, became furious at the loss of her prophets and swore to kill Elijah.

When Elijah heard about Jezebel's death threat, he became afraid. He was terribly discouraged, felt useless and despised his life. However, God was not moved by the threat of Jezebel. Rather He was impressed by the courage and confidence by which Elijah challenged King Ahab the prophets of Baal. God was impressed by his prophetic declaring about the coming drought and his prayers for restoration of rain. Those were good moves in the sight of God. Despite his momentary discouragement, God knew Elijah was capable of doing greater things. He was to appoint Elisha as his protégé, use his mantle to part River Jordan and drop his mantle and anointing for Elisha. Elijah has great value in the sight of God, no wonder he was taken to heaven by chariots of Fire. He did not have to die!

It appears God sometimes looks in us for those little insignificant acts, things that may be unrecognised and unappreciated by others to bless, promote and bring us to greater accomplishments. David was a shepherd boy looking after his father's sheep in the wilderness when his brothers were already in the battlefield. He was unappreciated by his brothers then. But God saw his caring heart and the bold and courageous move when he pursued the lion and the bear that tried to kill some of the sheep in his care. No wonder God trusted him that he would challenge Goliath and save his people from shame and ridicule.

God has confidence in you much more than people can imagine. He's seen those acts of mercy, kindness and generosity you have shown to others, even though people may not have noticed. He saw you when you visited the sick, needy, widow and fatherless. He wants you to appreciate who you are and who He is shaping you to be. You are worth more than gold.

CHAPTER THREE

THE POWER OF CHOICE

Perhaps the most powerful ability we all have as humans is our power of choice. We all have the ability to choose who we are supposed to be. I believe God has pre-destined each of us to accomplish a purpose. However, I strongly believe that God has also given each of us the ability to choose who we want to be, what we want to do with our lives, and what we do with our time and resources.

Our freedom of choice is our birth right. Knowing and exercising your power of choice gives you freedom. You have the power to consider your options and make your own choice. Others may give advice, suggestions, guidance, information, but the ultimate power of choice lies within you. You have the power to choose your thoughts, friends, environment, and different aspects of your life.

An awesome power has been welded in us by our creator - our ability to choose. Your ability to choose can empower you to overcome your past, re-invent yourself and secure a fulfilling and rewarding future. The decisions you make will ultimately determine your life and destiny.

Choices create Realities

Each of us make choices every day. We decide what is important to us and what is not important. Whether we are aware of it or not, the choices we make form our lives and our future. As Zig Zigar said "every choice you make has an end result". You are where you are today because of the choices you have made so far. The choices you are making right now and the choices you will continue to make will determine where you will be next year, in two years, three years, five years and more. If you continue to make wrong and unwise decisions, you may head towards failure, whereas right and wise choices repeated regularly are bound to lead to success. This is a cause and effect reality.

It's your choice

In life there are many things that will cry for your attention and although they may be legitimate, many of them may have little or no positive contribution to your dreams and purpose. You have a choice to give time, attention or energy to your dreams or to waste valuable time on things of lesser purpose. You have the ability to choose to study, read a helpful book, practice, go to the gym, attend the seminar, attend lectures, work on your project, pray or develop yourself mentally, emotionally and spiritually.

The Bible in Luke 10 verses 38 to 42 tells us about two sisters, Mary and Martha. Martha was cumbered with much serving while her sister Mary sat at the feet of Jesus, listening to His teachings. Realising that her sister did not join her in serving, Martha protested to Jesus, expecting Him to tell her sister to help her. Jesus responded to Martha by telling her that she was worried about many things while her sister had chosen a good part that cannot be taken away. In other words Jesus was telling Mary that each of them had the ability to choose what was important to them. As for Mary, she had chosen what was needful - to listen to the teachings of Jesus and to learn.

There is an interesting quote from William Clement Stone, a successful businessman, philanthropist and American self-help author. "You always do what you want to do. This is true for every act. You may say that you had to do something or you were forced to, but actually, whatever you do, you do it by choice, only you have the power to choose for yourself."

In 1 Samuel Chapter 13, the Bible gives account of King Saul's foolish decision after his appointment as the first King in Israel. In the second year of his reign, the Philistines - long-time enemies of Israel - amassed a great army of chariots, horsemen and foot soldiers to attack Israel. However, before Israel could go to battle, there was a need for sacrifices and prayers to God for help. The sacrifices had to be done by Samuel, who was the priest and prophet over the nation. Samuel had promised King Saul that he would come to Gilgal within seven days to intercede for the nation and make the necessary sacrifices for Israel to be spiritually prepared for the battle.

King Saul waited seven days according to set time by Samuel, but Samuel has not yet arrived and some of the Israelites soldiers were going back home. When King Saul saw that his army was becoming smaller and smaller, he became impatient and decided he could not wait any longer for Samuel. He decided to offer the sacrifices. No sooner were the sacrifices completed that Samuel arrived. Samuel did not approve of the King's action as he was not a priest and only priests were to offer sacrifices in accordance with the law of God as prescribed in Leviticus 6:8-13.

King Saul had no business doing what only a priest should do. However, he excused his decision and action by saying he felt compelled to offer the sacrifice because Samuel was late and some of the soldiers were leaving. Despite the King's excuses Samuel pronounced God's judgement. The King's actions were foolish and wilful disobedience for which he would eventually lose his kingship. Though King Saul felt compelled, he was not supposed to be ruled by his feelings. Although Samuel was late, the King could have trusted God's wisdom. However, he blamed Samuel for his foolish decision. His excuse could be interpreted as this. "Samuel, if you had come earlier, I wouldn't have felt the need to do this. I blame you for my decision and action. You made me offer the sacrifices, even though I did not want to do it". But it was the King's choice. Likewise you are responsible for your decisions, choices and actions even if people or other external factors may influence you. It's your choice.

Taking Responsibility for your Choices

So many people make decisions without thinking about the potential consequences of their choices. They do whatever it takes to push their personal agendas regardless of the potential impact of their decisions and actions on themselves and others. However, they are not willing to face the consequences of their actions. They lay blame on everyone else and refuse to accept responsibility for their actions. Nicolas Roquefort–Villeneuve, a relationship counsellor, commented that "the choice to lay blame on someone else is a reflection of someone's refusal to truthfully look at his or her own self. And such refusal is the mark of an individual who lives inside a constant lie about what he or she truly is."

Concern yourself more with accepting responsibility for your choices and actions instead of assigning blames. When you place responsibility for your choices and actions on others, you are not behaving in a Christ–like manner. Your choices and actions may not just affect you but can have great consequences on others including generations after you, good or bad.

In the Bible the story of Adam and Eve, the first couple on earth illustrates this truth. At creation God planted a garden in a place called Eden where He made all kinds of trees that were good for food to grow. He placed Adam and his wife Eve in the garden to enjoy the fruits of His creation. They were given free will. However, God gave them specific instructions about the trees in the garden. They could eat the fruit of every tree except one, the fruit of the tree of knowledge of good and evil. God warned them that eating the fruit of the tree will result in death. Sadly they disobeyed God. When tempted by Satan, Eve made the wrong choice, ate the fruit of the forbidden tree and also gave her husband to eat some.

Although Eve blamed Satan, and Adam blamed Eve, the truth is that each chose to eat the forbidden fruit. Their disobedience was not without consequences. Their blame games could not shift the consequences of their wrong choices. The consequences were immediate and far-reaching. After eating the forbidden fruit Adam and Eve experienced unpleasant feelings of guilt. They had an uncomfortable awareness of being naked and felt ashamed. They were driven out of the garden, lost their connection with God and their life expectancy was reduced. They no longer had all their needs met with ease. They had to struggle to get food, drink, shelter and safety. Eve and all mothers would have to suffer painful childbirth and no human being would live on earth forever.

As a result of disobedience, Adam and Eve distorted their nature which had been made in the very image and likeness of God. They became incapable of perfect obedience. All mankind fell from grace with them. Every human being is now born into a fallen and fragmented world, a world infected with sin, sickness, suffering and death. A terrible curse was released on earth because of their disobedience! The evil that we see in the world today came as a result of their disobedience. But thanks be to Jesus Christ, who made a choice to obey the will of God by dying on the cross, thereby paying the price for our salvation and redemption. Following disobedience of Adam and Eve, God in His love and mercy offered forgiveness, though a blood sacrifice was required. God decided that His Son, Jesus would be that sacrifice. Jesus took the form of man, born by a virgin, lived on earth and eventually paid the ultimate price by shedding His blood on the cross of Calvary. Jesus had a choice not to surrender to the crucifixion, but He chose to lay down His life as a sacrificial offering to redeem mankind from the curse of disobedience of Adam and Eve.

Power to Respond

You may not have a choice regarding everything that happens in your life, your circumstances or how others treat you. But you always have the power to choose how to respond.

The late Viktor Emil Frankl, a professor of neurology and psychiatry at the University of Vienna made a profound statement "Between stimulus and response there is a space. In that space is our power to choose our response. In our response lies our growth and our freedom". In his statement he implies that people often react without thinking. We frequently don't choose our behaviours so much as just act them out. He observed that we don't need to accept such reflex reactions. Instead, we can learn to notice that there is a "space" before we react. He suggests that we can grow and change and be different if we can learn to recognise, increase, and make use of this "space". With such awareness, we can find freedom from the dictates of both external and internal pressures. And with that, we can find inner happiness.

Many people do not realise they have the ability to respond appropriately to situations. They react rather than respond. There is a difference between reacting and responding. Usually people react without thinking. Reaction is often based on fear and insecurities. People react with anger, defensiveness, hatred, bitterness, disgust and all kinds of negative emotions. Responding on the other hand is more thoughtful and rational. It is a conscious choice. You take control. Responding gives you command over situations.

Viktor Frankl observed further that "Forces beyond your control can take away everything you possess except one thing, your freedom to choose how you will respond to situations."

In the Bible, a whole book is devoted to the story about the trial and restoration of a man by the name Job. All was going well with Job. He had it all, a large family, wealth and blessings of every kind imaginable. In Job chapter 1:2-3, the Bible says *"He had seven sons and three daughters, and he owned seven thousand sheep, three thousand camels, five hundred yoke of oxen and five hundred donkeys, and had a large number of servants. He was the greatest man among all the people of the East."*

God initiated a conversation about Job with Satan. God bragged that there was no one on earth like Job. God attested that Job was "blameless, fears God and shuns evil." Satan, however, challenged Job's sincerity. He insisted that Job only fears God for the favour and protection he enjoyed from God and that the moment God withdrew all these blessings, Job would curse God to His face. As you may be aware, Satan is the "accuser of the brethren". He specialises in using accusations, criticisms, condemnation and lies to discredit God's beloved people. He is also described in the Bible as a thief and robber. He seeks to destroy every good thing that God is doing and also rob God's people of blessings by causing sickness, diseases, losses, misfortunes, struggles and hardships.

Satan demanded that God permitted him to test Job. However, God set out to prove to Satan that Job was not righteous just because he was blessed, but out of the integrity of his heart. God therefore allowed Satan to attack Job's possession; however, he would not allow Satan to kill Job. Satan therefore went on a rampage. Job lost just about everything; his sheep, his oxen, his camels, his servants, and all of his sons and daughters but he did not lose his faith in God. Despite his losses, Job praised God. He said: "Naked I came from my mother's womb, and naked shall I return there. The Lord gave, and the LORD has taken away; Blessed be the name of the Lord." Despite his losses, Job did not sin nor charge God with wrong. But that was not the end of his trial.

Satan put more pressure on Job by afflicting him with painful sores all over his body. His suffering was so much that his wife even told him to curse God and die. But Job would not react negatively to God. The Bible records that in all Job's suffering he *"did not sin nor charge God with wrong"*. He did not react with anger, accusations or bitterness towards God. He made a choice to praise God irrespective of pressure from circumstances and pressure from family and friends. Eventually God restored Job's fortune and blessed him with much more greatness, riches and family.

You may be wondering how can I respond rather than react to situations? It takes willingness and determination. Here are few suggestions that you may find helpful.

➤ Pause to reflect on the problem, situation or circumstance. This may take a few seconds, a few hours, days, weeks or months. If the situation requires an immediate action, take a deep breath before responding.

➤ Consider your options, alternatives and potential consequences of your actions. Recognise that you have a choice. Often people react because they assume they do not have any other options. When you recognise that you have options and choice, you'll be empowered to make better decisions.

➤ Be willing to learn and accept responsibilities for the outcome of your choices and actions.

It's Never too Late

Making choices is not always easy. Even with the best intentions, we can still make wrong choices. Certainly this may lead to painful experiences, however, it is possible to learn from our wrong choices and make every effort to correct it.

The Bible describes in 2 Samuel chapter 6 how King David and the Israelites brought the Ark of God from Baalah in Judah to Jerusalem. The Ark was the centre of worship in the tabernacle and in the temple. It was where priests went into the Holy of Holies to offer sacrifices to God for the sins of the people. The Ark represented the manifest presence of God. However, the Ark was captured by the Philistines in a battle between them and the Israelites. After its capture, the presence of the Ark was causing problems to the Philistines, so they returned the Ark to Israel.

After some time King David decided to bring the Ark to Jerusalem, the capital of Israel. The first attempt to bring back the Ark was a colossal failure. King David and the people of Israel made a wrong decision. They followed the same method as the Philistines when they sent the Ark back to Israel by putting it on a new cart drawn by the oxen. This decision resulted in tragedy. The Ark was not to be touched. Poles for carrying the Ark were placed through rings which had been attached to the Ark. When they came to a place called the "threshing floor of Chidon," the oxen shook the Ark. Uzza, one the priests' son reached out and touched the Ark to keep it from stumbling. He died instantly. Although his motive may have been sincere, he was wrong. His human solution to correct an incident brought on by wrong-doing could not be justified in the eyes of God. Back in the time of Moses, the Lord had instructed that the Ark must be carried on the shoulders of consecrated priesthood.

King David decided to move the Ark a second time. He now knew how the Ark should be transported and so instructed the priests to carry the Ark on their shoulders. This time he got it right. The Ark was moved the way God instructed. Therefore, the second attempt was successful and there was rejoicing and jubilations by the Israelites.

Stephen Covey in his book *"The 8th Habit"* states that "Everyone chooses one of two roads in life. One is the broad, well- travelled road to mediocrity, the other road to greatness and meaning. The path to mediocrity straitjackets human potential. The path to greatness unleashes and realises human potential. The path to mediocrity is the quick-fix, short approach to life. The path to greatness is a process of sequential growth from inside out. Travellers on the lower path to mediocrity live out the cultural 'software' of ego, indulgence, scarcity, comparison, competitiveness and victimism. Travellers on the upper path to greatness rise above negative cultural influences and choose to become the creative force of their lives."

You probably have read about the parable of the prodigal son narrated by Jesus in the Bible in Luke chapter 15. According to the parable, a man had two sons. The younger son put pressure on his father to give him his share of the estate, although the father was still alive. So the father divided his property between the two sons and gave the younger one his share. The younger son took all he got and travelled to a far country and squandered his wealth on wasteful spending.

After spending everything there was a famine in the whole country and he began to be in need. He could no longer afford basic human necessities. He took a job feeding pigs. His condition was so bad that he wished he could eat from the pods that the pigs fed on, but no one gave him anything. He came to his senses and realised that even the servants working for his father back home had enough, while he was starving to death. He made a choice. He decided to return to his father and ask for forgiveness. His father welcomed him back gladly, dressed him with the best robe and made a feast to celebrate his return.

This story illustrates the truth of the statement by Stephen Covey. The younger son was travelling on "the path of mediocrity and short term approach to life". He was living out of indulgence that led to scarcity and humiliation. Despite his humiliating and downgrading circumstances he had the ability to choose, to change paths. He decided to leave behind the life of mediocrity and travelled back home on a path that restored him to greatness.

Maybe you have been travelling on the path of mediocrity all your life, like that younger son. You can also change your life by making decisions to move to the path of greatness that you really belong to. You can rise above your disappointments, failures, foolishness and pride to a path that unleashes your potential. No matter how long you have walked the path of mediocrity, you can still change paths. It's never too late. Yes, it's never too late to make a U-turn, it's never too late to make better choices. It's never too late to reclaim your life and the dreams back. It's never too late to make a fresh start. You have the power to change your life forever and live true to the person you are created to be.

CHAPTER FOUR

MAXIMISE YOUR POTENTIAL

In 1 Timothy 4: 14-15, the Bible records a letter written by Apostle Paul to Timothy, who was a young Pastor at that time. In his letter Paul wrote *"Do not neglect your gift, which was given you through prophecy when council of elders laid their hands on you. Practice these things; immerse yourself in them, so that all may see your progress"* *(ESV).*

In another letter to Timothy, he wrote *"I remind you to stir up the gift of God which is in you through the laying on of my hand. For God had not given us a spirit of fear, but of power, and of love and of a sound mind"* (2 Timothy 1:6-7 NKJV). In these letters Paul was reminding Timothy that God has deposited a gift in him and potential that needed to be used.

There is greatness in you. God has put in you potential, gifts, talents and abilities that can help you make positive contributions here on earth.

In Judges Chapters 13 to 16, the Bible gives an account of extraordinary accomplishments of Samson, a man with supernatural strength. God sent an Angel to Samson's mother before she became pregnant. He told her that she would be pregnant with a special son. He should never cut his hair, eat grapes or drink wine, or touch dead bodies. His purpose was to save the Israelites from the Philistines. She became pregnant and gave birth to Samson. As he grew up he realised that he had a special gift: he was incredibly strong. As he got older, he was able to kill a lion with his bare hands and a thousand Philistines (enemies) with the jawbone of a donkey. That was incredible strength!

John the Baptist, the cousin and forerunner of our Lord Jesus Christ was given the ability to preach a message of repentance for the forgiveness of sins. He was filled with the Holy Spirit, while he was still a foetus in his mother's womb. As a child, he sensed his call to be a forerunner to Jesus Christ. He devoted his time in the wilderness to fellowshipping with God and developing his spiritual gifts and abilities.

David had the ability and skills to play musical instrument from his youth. He was invited to play music for King Saul when he was being tormented by evil spirits, which calmed his soul. The book of Psalms in the Bible was written by David, which was also testament of his poetic abilities.

In Exodus 31:1-16, Bezalel was said to be highly gifted as a workman, showing great skill and originality in engraving precious metals, stones and in wood-carving. He was endowed by God to direct the construction of the tent of meeting, as instructed by God to Moses.

We all have seeds of greatness. Some people are great entertainers, artists, sportsmen, communicators, negotiators, investors, while others excel at inventing things, solving complex problems, medical or scientific research, or other forms of human endeavours.

The parable of the talents is one of the stories Jesus told to teach spiritual and life lessons. According to the parable, a wealthy man decided to travel to a far country. Before he embarked on his journey, he called his servants and entrusted his talents with them. He gave five talents to one servant; to another he gave two talents and one to the third servant. He gave the talents to each according to their ability. The servant with five talents traded with his talents and gained five more talent. The servant with two talents also traded with his talents and gained two more talents. But the servant with one talent buried his talent in the ground.

When the master returned from his journey, he was eager to know what the servants have done with the talents he gave them. The servant with five talents said to the master "You trusted me with five talents and I made five more". The master was very pleased with him and said" Well done, good and faithful servant! You have been faithful in a few things. I will put you in charge of many things. Enter into the joy of your master". The servant with two talents also said to his master" you trusted me with two talents and I made two more". The master was also pleased with him and said "You have been faithful in a few things. I will put you in charge of many things. Enter into the joy of your master."

However, the servant with one talent brought the same talent to the master and said" I was afraid to lose any of it, so I decided to bury it and keep it safe". The master was obviously not impressed with the servant. He said to him" you slothful servant; at least you could have taken the money to the bank and could have had some interest from it". Immediately he took the talent from him and gave it to the first servant who had five talents. The profitable servants were praised and rewarded by their master.

The talents in the parable refer to money. However, talents in this story can also mean gifts and abilities. Each of us have been given special gifts and abilities by God, though everyone's ability is different. If you use your gifts and abilities, you will certainly be rewarded by God. He will give you more opportunities and grace to keep doing the things you are good at doing. However, if you ignore or refuse to use you gifts, you stand the risk of losing rewards that God intends for you.

Benefits of Maximising Your Potential

One of the greatest things you can do that will give you joy and fulfilment is to discover, develop, exercise and maximise your potential.

Your potential will bring you rewards. By recognising and developing your God-given talents and abilities, you can earn great rewards. According to the parable of the talents, the master rewarded the servants who used their talents profitably with praises and the opportunity to gain more. Rewards that can come to you when you develop and exercise your potential can be in different forms. Recognition, honour, wealth, favour, influence and promotion are some of the rewards you can enjoy.

Andy Murray, a Scottish professional tennis player, stated playing tennis at the age of three. He entered his first competitive tournament at age five. He won a gold medal at the 2012 London Olympic Games by defeating Switzerland's Roger Federer in straight sets, making him the first British singles champion in over 100 years. In the same year he won the US Open grand slam in New York, making him the first British player since 1977, and British man since 1936, to win a grand slam singles tournament. He was awarded an OBE (Order of the British Empire) by Prince William at Buckingham Palace for his achievements in 2012. Following another grand slam victory in Wimbledon 2013, he was awarded the freedom of Stirling, the greatest civic honour the Stirling Council can confer in

April 2014. In the same year, the University of Stirling also awarded him an honorary doctorate degree in recognition of his outstanding contributions to tennis.

Boxing legend, Mohammed Ali, generally considered amongst the greatest heavyweights in sports history, has received one of the world's most prestigious awards. He was first introduced to boxing by Joe Martin, a Louiseville police officer and boxing coach. When Mohammed Ali was 12 years old, he and his friend went to the Columbia Auditorium to help themselves to free hot dogs and popcorn available for visitors of Louisville Home Show. After finishing eating, they went back to get their bicycles only to discover that Ali's bicycle had been stolen. Furious, he went to the basement of Columbia Auditorium to report the crime to Police Officer Joe Martin. He told Joe he was going to "whip" whoever stole his bicycle. Joe told him, he better learn how to box first. That statement launched Ali to unlock his boxing potential.

Joe Martin became his first trainer at a local gym. Young Ali trained under him for 6 years. He won 100 of 108 amateur fights. After advancing through the amateur ranks, he won a gold medal in the 1960 Olympic Games in Rome at the age of 18. After winning the Olympic medal, he began a professional boxing career under the guidance of Louiseville Sponsoring Group, a syndicate composed of 11 wealthy white men. In February 1964, Ali became the heavyweight boxing champion of the world when he beat Sonny Liston, at the age of 22.

Ali had unique qualities that helped him through his fights. He was quick, strong-willed and witty. In one of his pre-fight interviews against Liston, Ali declared he would "float like a butterfly and sting like a bee". At the time of his retirement in 1981 he had a career record of

57 wins (37 by knockouts) and 5 defeats. He was the first person in history to win the heavyweight champion title three times. He was diagnosed with Parkinson disease in 1984. Despite his diagnosis, his sensational boxing career and style has inspired many boxers of later generations. In 1990 he was inducted into International Boxing Hall of fame. He had the honour of lighting the Olympic torch to open the games in 1996 in Atlanta. In 1999, he was crowned 'Sportsman of the Century'. In 2005, he was awarded the Presidential Medal of Freedom, the highest US civilian honour. Most recently he was named flag bearer at the 2012 London Olympic Games, though he was too ill to carry the flag. However, he stood in front of it.

It is encouraging to know that anyone who is determined to unlock and maximise their potential can come to the limelight no matter their family, cultural or racial background.

Alex Amosu, a Luxury designer was born in London to Nigerian parents. He started earning money at the age of 12 by doing paper rounds earning £10.00 a week. He undertook a business start-up course at college at the age of 19, after which he wrote a business plan which was impressive to the Prince's Trust. The Trust awarded him a grant to start a cleaning business which generated about £4,000 a month.

In 2000, young Alex sent his brother a ringtone he had made using the composing facility of his Nokia phone. The tune was "Big Pimpin" by American rapper Jay Z. His brother's phone went off at college and it was an instant hit. 21 of his brother's classmates wanted to have the ringtone on their phones. At that time most people only had the ringtone that came with their phones. Alex immediately put on his entrepreneur cap, charged his brother's classmates £1.00 each for the ringtone instead of giving it out free. He made £21 in profit. He thought "That's fantastic, what would happen if I make 100 or more ringtones?" He did some research and found out that only two companies were making ringtones in the UK, both focusing on pop music based ringtone. So he decided to set up an R&B ringtone making business. He started his business at his father's house, advertised his business in several universities and started earning £6.00 a day which grew aggressively and he was able to earn enough money to rent an office within four months. In the first year, his business turned over £1 million and generated a turnover of £6 million in four years. He sold off the business in 2004 using the proceeds to launch his latest venture, Amosu Costum.

He has flair for creating the most exclusive and exquisite products targeting celebrities and rich people who are able to afford them. The price tags of his diamond encrusted handset range from £5,000 to £1 million.

In 2009, Alex Amosu created a bespoke suit which earned him a name in the Guinness Book of Record as the designer of the most expensive suit in the world. The suit was a one-off creation which took over 80 hours to complete. The fabric of the suit was made from Vicuña, a rare South American wild animal, related to the camel, which only produces enough wool for shearing every three years; and qiviuk, the world's most expensive wool, gathered from Arctic muskox. The suit features 5,000 individual stitches which were done manually. The buttons were made of 18-carat gold and pave set diamonds. I think it was an amazing suit! Would you like to own it? Sorry it's too late; it was sold in 2009 to an anonymous buyer for the price of £70,000.

Adding another bejewelled phone to his ever-growing list of luxury and customised products, Alex Amosu created the most expensive Blackberry 18-carat gold Curve in the same year. Just 24 hours after Apple announced the iPhone 6 in September 2014, Alex Amosu created a customised version, in solid 18-carat gold encrust with 6,127 diamonds. It sold quickly to another anonymous buyer at a staggering price of £1.7 million!

You may be thinking that spending so much on luxury items is very materialistic and unnecessary. Well, it's all relative. Alex Amosu targets his high end, luxury custom products to customers who want them and are willing to pay the asking prices without feeling the pinch. I think his drive, initiative and business acumen is commendable. Many young people have sabotaged their potentials through drugs, robbery, laziness or other destructive lifestyles.

Alex Amosu was named among the top 100 most influential black Britons in 2009. To recognise his achievements, he was invited to 10 Downing Street, the home of British Prime Minister to celebrate Black History Month. Alex also has a keen interest in working with charities; he organised Free Ringtone Day, where he donated the revenue from over 75,000 orders in one day to Teenage Cancer Trust. He had also donated part of the funds received from his bespoke tailoring services to children's medical research.

Are you wondering if I am one of Amosu's marketing executives? Not really. The essence of including his success story in this book is to inspire and awaken the giant within you. You probably have in you one of the best songs that the world has never heard, or one of the best books that the world has never read. Or maybe you have one of the most thriving business ideas, or one of the most needed scientific and medical breakthroughs the world is waiting for. Don't despise your little beginnings. You probably have one of the most amazing technological and innovative idea the world has never seen. If you unlock and maximise your potential, you'll be amazed at the heights you can attain. God will see to it that the world recognises your contributions. If I hear about your achievement, I promise, I will publish it to inspire and encourage others too.

Are you thinking that age is no longer on your side? Maybe you are in your 40s, 50s or 60s and thinking it's too late to unlock or maximise your potential. Don't be discouraged. It's never too late. Greatness has no age limit.

Colonel Sanders, founder of the well-known fast food chicken restaurant, Kentucky Fried Chicken - more popularly known as KFC - was well over 60 years old when he founded the hugely successful restaurant chain. Prior to this, he was selling fried chicken from a roadside restaurant in Corbin, Kentucky. At the time he started franchising his chicken recipe at the age of 65, he was living off a monthly social security check of 105 dollars and some savings. However, he decided that he was not going to settle for a quiet retirement. He maximised his potential by devoting his efforts to franchising his chicken concept. By 1964, Colonel Sanders had 600 franchise outlets for his chicken across the United States and Canada. The company's rapid expansion became overwhelming for ageing Sanders and he eventually sold the business for $2 million at the age of 70. By the time of his death in December 1980 at age 90, there were estimated 6,000 KFC outlets in 48 countries worldwide with $2 billion of sales annually.

The Legacy of Colonel Sanders lives on with KFC restaurants all over the world. KFC now stretches worldwide with more than 13,000 restaurants in more than 80 countries serving up Colonel Sanders's original chicken recipe. Have you been to any KFC restaurant? You would have seen Colonel Sander's face outside the restaurant and on the chicken buckets. Sander's face remains the official face of KFC and appears on the logo.

On May 14 2007, Nola Ochs became a Guinness World Record holder as the world's oldest graduate. She graduated from Fort Hays State University in Kansas at the age of 95. She earned a general studies degree with an emphasis in history. I read that she graduated alongside her 21 year old granddaughter. Nola started her first college class in 1930, but got side-tracked by farm work and the demands of raising her children and grandchildren. She said "I live in a farm. I was a mother and grandmother, I had plenty to do. But the yearning didn't go away." Nola took college courses again after her husband died in 1972 and finished her degree.

After graduation, Princes Cruises hired her as a guest lecturer on a nine-day cruise where she shared her personal experience and stories of life on a farmland. For most people, a bachelor's degree might have been enough accomplishment at that age, but not for Nola. She started pursuing her Master's degree in Liberal Studies. In May 2010 at the age of 98, Nola received her master's degree making her the oldest person to receive the degree. She took a job as a graduate teaching assistant. She celebrated her 100th birthday in November 2011 and started writing her first book.

Nola's achievement is a great inspiration as well as challenge to both young and older people who think they can be limited by age. Her commitment, courage and resilience helped her unlock and maximise her potential, even in her old age. She once said "I don't dwell on my age. It might limit what I can do. As long as I have my mind and health, age is a number". Friend, don't limit yourself because of your age. You can still unlock and maximise your potential. You can do great things. With God all things are possible.

Anna Mary Moses, better known by the nickname Grandma Moses, was a renowned American artist. She began painting in her late 70s after abandoning a career in embroidery due to arthritis. Although she could no longer hold a needle, she could hold a brush. Drawing from her memory, her paintings provide nostalgic glimpses of rural American life. Her first few paintings sold for between $3 and $5 depending on the size. As her fame increased, her works were sold for between $8,000 and $10,000. Grandma Moses had appeared on magazine covers, televisions and several documentary of her life. At the age of 88, a magazine named her as "Young Woman of the Year." She died in December 1961 at 101 years. After her death, her works was exhibited in several large travelling exhibitions in the US and abroad. Her paintings were used to publicise American holidays like Thanksgiving, Christmas and Mother's Day. Her paintings have also been reproduced on Hallmark greeting cards, tiles, fabrics and ceramics. In November 2006, her work named 'Sugaring Off' sold for $1.2 million. In her autograph titled '*My Life History*' published in 1952, Grandma Moses stated "I look back on my life like a good day's work, it was done and I feel satisfied with it. I was happy and content, I knew nothing better and made the best out of what life offered. And life is what we make it, always has been, always will be."

Looking back at your life, do you feel dissatisfied? Are you feeling hopeless about the future? Don't lose hope, it's never too late. You can still turn it around. You can still unlock your potential, you can still achieve your dreams, and you can accomplish any goal you set for yourself. But you may need to feel young in your mind and see age as just a number rather than a barrier. You have to feel young and strong in your mind, like Caleb who at the age of 85 was willing to possess the inheritance God promised him when he was just 45 years old.

Sometimes it can be so tempting to feel helpless and accept limitations and status quo due to infirmity, disability or any other kind of circumstances beyond human control. Many people believe their infirmity or disability can hold them back from unlocking and maximising their potential. The devil often works overtime to sabotage greatness by afflicting people with circumstances or infirmity so that they will not reach their God-ordained potential. The good news is that there are thousands of people who through God's grace and determination have unlocked and maximised their God-given potential, against all odds.

Moses, the great Hebrew leader and prophet whom God used mightily many years ago to deliver and lead the Israelites out of Egypt, initially protested when God called him out to be a leader. Moses probably did realise at that time that God's grace was sufficient to help him unlock his leadership potential. Moses pointed out his limitation of speech impairment to God and suggested that He find a more talented speaker who would effectively lead the Israelites out of Egypt.

The Bible records the conversation between God and Moses in Exodus 4:10-11 (NIV).

"Moses said to the Lord, "Pardon your servant, Lord. I have never been eloquent, neither in the past nor since you have spoken to your servant. I am slow of speech and tongue."

The Lord said to him, "Who gave human beings their mouths? Who makes them deaf or mute? Who gives them sight or makes them blind? Is it not I, the Lord? Now go; I will help you speak and will teach you what to say."

Through God's grace and the assistance of Aaron, Moses was able to confront Pharaoh, the terrorising King who kept the Israelites under bondage for several years. God performed many signs and wonders through Moses and he effectively delivered and led over 600,000 Israelites out of Egypt in the middle of the night to the Promised Land. The story of Moses' life shows he was incredibly gifted in many areas. He was a humble leader, intercessor, judge and a great writer. He was instrumental in establishing the well-known Ten Commandments of God in the Bible. He is also believed to have written the first five books of the Old Testament.

It can be a struggle for individuals with disabilities or other infirmities to live normal lives or purse their dreams. However, the grace of God has empowered many to live normal lives, unlock their potentials and accomplish great things in all spheres of human endeavours.

Blade runner, Oscar Pistorius was diagnosed with a rare medical condition known as "Fibular Hemimelia" shortly after he was born. Consequently both of his legs were amputated below the knee when he was 11 months old. Despite his disability, he grew up playing a wide range of able bodied sports such as rugby, water polo, wrestling, tennis and sprinting.

At the 2011 World Championships in Athletics, Oscar Pistoris became the first amputee to win an able-bodied world track medal. At the 2012 Summer Olympics, he became the first double leg amputee to participate in the Olympics when he entered the men's 400 metres and 4 × 400 metres relay races. At the 2012 Summer Paralympics, Pistorius won gold medals in the men's 400-metre race and in the 4 × 100 metres relay, setting world records in both events.

Nick Vujicic, a Christian evangelist and motivational speaker was born with tetra-amelia syndrome, a rare disorder characterised by the absence of all four limbs. As a child, he struggled mentally and emotionally as well as physically, but eventually came to terms with his disability. At the age of seventeen he started his own non-profit organisation, Life Without Limbs. Nick now gives motivational speeches worldwide which focus on living with a disability, hope and finding meaning in life.

When you embrace the grace of God, you can live a life without limits and accomplish great things despite adversity or human limitations. I must not forget to mention the accomplishments of my great uncle Dr TM Aluko. His life and accomplishments also exemplified the grace of God. I was privileged to live with him and his wife years ago when I was studying at the Law school in Lagos, Nigeria. Dr TM Aluko was a Nigerian novelist, engineer and lecturer. He studied Civil Engineering and Town Planning at the University of London, held a number of administrative posts in Nigeria, including Director of Works in Western Nigeria, and was a University lecturer. Most significantly, he was a creative writer. He began unlocking his creative writing potential in the 1940s when he started writing short stories. He won the British Council short story prize in 1945. The publication of his first novel *"One *man, One wife"* in 1959 brought him considerable public attention in Africa and overseas. Since then he had written many other novels which enjoyed wide acclaim in Africa and among the most widely studied in Nigerian schools. These include *"One man, One Machete"*, *"Kinsman & Foreman"*, *"Chief, the Honourable Minister"*, *"His Worshipful Majesty"* and *"Wrong Ones In the Dock"*. In 1963, he received the Officer of British Empire award, followed by Order of Nigerian award in 1964.

Dr T.M. Aluko suffered from a stroke, on August 27, 1987 at the age of 69, leaving him paralysed on his right side. This almost ended his writing career as his writing hand was also paralysed. The prospect of continuing to write became dim as he could not dictate his works. However, where there is a will, God always brings a way. His loving wife, fondly referred to as "Aunty Bisi" by my mum, encouraged him to try his left hand. Although this nudge of encouragement got him on a difficult start, indeed it was a fresh start for him. Afterwards he went on to write other well-known books. In November 2009, at the age of 91, he celebrated the 50th anniversary of his first novel, *"One Man, One Wife"*. At the celebration, he unveiled another book entitled *"Our Born-Again President"*. Sadly he passed away in May 2010, His death was a major loss to Nigerian and African literature. Friend, don't ignore, limit or abandon your God-given, gifts, talents and abilities. They can bring you to significance and recognition.

Joseph was recognised and promoted by the King when he used his God-given ability to interpret the King's dream. According to the Bible in Genesis 41:38, the King said *"Can we find such a man as this in whom is the spirit of God?"* This was a significant recognition that turned the life of Joseph totally around. He became second in command to the King throughout the land of Egypt.

Leona Lewis achieved international recognition when she won the third series of The UK X Factor in 2006. She would not have come to the limelight if she had neglected or abandoned her passion for singing and song writing.

The Bible states in Proverbs 22:29 (AMP) *"Do you see a man diligent in his business? He shall stand before kings, he will not stand before obscure men."*

The word 'diligent' means constant in effort, steady and persistent in doing something. People who identify and work consistently to develop and maximise their potentials and talents come to significant recognition in the world.

Your potential will boost your self-esteem and self-confidence. When you recognise what you are good at and focus your attention on developing and maximising it, you feel a sense of self confidence. With time and practice, you'll become more skilled and proficient, which will surely cause a sense of pride and fulfilment at what you're able to achieve.

Your potential will help you understand, appreciate and celebrate your uniqueness. Some people may look like you, talk like you or walk like you. But no one is quite like you. You were born original.

Your potential is your opportunity to make your mark in the world. Discovering and developing you potential and ability will help you make a positive impact and contribute to solving problems on earth.

Enemies of Potential

Ignorance

The worst enemy of human potential is ignorance. It is the inward void that starves people of relevant knowledge and information. It is like a blank space in a person's mental map. Many people are unaware of the greatness within them. They have talents and abilities that are dormant, waiting to be activated. However, ignorance has hidden these possibilities from their reach. If you do not know or recognise your potential, your ignorance will hold you back. Ignorance will rob you of many privileges, advantages, opportunities and benefits that rightfully belong to you.

There once was a man whose lifelong dream was to board a cruise ship and sail the Mediterranean. He dreamed of walking the streets of Rome, Athens and Istanbul. He saved every penny until he had enough for his passage. He brought an extra suitcase filled with cans of beans, boxes of crackers, and bags of powdered lemonade, and that is what he lived on every day.

He would have loved to take part in the many activities offered on the ship: working out in the gym, playing miniature golf, and swimming in the pool. He envied those who went to movies, shows, and cultural presentations. And, oh, how he yearned for only a taste of the amazing food he saw on the ship — every meal appeared to be a feast! But the man wanted to spend so very little money that he didn't participate in any of these. He was able to see the cities he had longed to visit, but for the most part of the journey, he stayed in his cabin and ate only his humble food.

On the last day of the cruise, a crew member asked him which of the farewell parties he would be attending. It was then that the man learned that not only the farewell party but almost everything else on board the cruise ship — the food, the entertainment, all the activities — had been included in the price of his ticket! Too late the man realised that he had been living far beneath his privileges.

That is how ignorance works. It blindfolds, limits and moves people far from opportunities and privileges that are actually within their reach. It makes princes to stay as paupers, it makes masters to be slaves, nobles to be peasants. No wonder the Bible records in Ecclesiastes 10:7 that servants ride on horses and princes walk on earth like servants.

Ignorance is a deceiver. It can make you believe less about yourself and keep you in a wrong environment.

There is an old story about a farmer who found an eagle's egg. He put it under a hen and soon the egg hatched. The young eagle grew up with all the other chickens and whatever they did, the eagle did too. He thought he was a chicken. Since the chickens could only fly for a short distance, the eagle also learnt to fly a short distance. Because he thought that was all he could do, that was all he was able to do.

One day the eagle saw a bird flying high above him. He was very impressed. "Who is that?", he asked the chickens around him. "That's an eagle, the king of the birds." replied a chicken. "He is the king of the sky. But we belong here on earth, we are just chickens", she continued. So the eagle continued to behave like a chicken, for he thought he was. Finally he died, never knowing nor experiencing life that could have been his.

Sadly, cemeteries are filled with talented people, both young and old, who died without ever releasing their full potential. Many died depressed, destitute, bitter and frustrated about life, never experiencing the joy and satisfaction of a fulfilled and purposeful life.

I believe you are holding this book because God wants to open your eyes to see the treasures and greatness that lies within you. I pray that as you continue reading this book you will come to the realisation of the treasures within you.

Wrong Associations

Many people have not been able to realise and maximise their true potential because of their associations. You may not realise it, but the people you spend most of your time with influence your thoughts, mindset, habits and behaviours. If people around you are negative and don't aspire for great things, they will surely hold you back. That's why it's important to re-assess the people you allow into your life. Are they motivating or demotivating you? Are they elevating you or bringing you down? Are they strengthening or empowering your life? Are they proactive or reactive people?

Colin Powell, a retired four-star general in the American army, once said "The less you associate with some people, the more your life will improve. Any time you tolerate mediocrity in others, it increases your mediocrity. An important attribute in successful people is their impatience with negative thinking and negative acting people. As you grow, your associates will change. Some of your friends will not want you to go on. They will want you to stay where they are. Friends that don't help you climb will want you to crawl. Your friends will stretch your vision or choke your dream. Those that don't increase you will eventually decrease you."

Very true, if you truly desire to unlock and maximise your potential, I suggest you consider the statement by General Powell carefully.

There is another version of the story of the chickens and eagle that is encouraging. A naturalist was visiting a farmer one day and was surprised to see a beautiful eagle in the farmer's chicken coop. He asked "Why in the world have you got this eagle living with the chickens?" "Well", answered the farmer, "I found him when he was little and raised him in there with the chickens. He doesn't know any better, he thinks he is a chicken." The naturalist was dumbfounded. The eagle was pecking the grain and drinking from the watering can. The eagle kept his eyes on the ground and strutted around in circles, looking every inch a big, oversized chicken. "Doesn't he ever try to spread his wings and fly out of there?" he asked. The farmer replied "No, I doubt he ever will, he doesn't know what it means to fly". In response to the farmer's comments he said "Well, let me take him out and do a few experiments with him. The farmer agreed, but assured him that he was wasting his time.

The naturalist lifted the bird to the top of the chicken coop fence and said "Fly!" He pushed the reluctant bird off the fence and it fell to the ground in a pile of dusty feathers. Next, the undaunted researcher took the ruffled eagle to the farmer's hay loft and spread its wings before tossing it high in the air with the command "FLY!" The frightened bird shrieked and fell ungraciously to the barnyard floor where it resumed pecking the ground in search of its dinner. He picked up the eagle again and decided to give it one more chance in a more appropriate environment, away from the bad examples of a chicken lifestyle. He set the docile bird on the front seat of his pickup truck next to him and headed for the highest butte in the country.

After a lengthy and sweaty climb to the crest of the butte with the bird tucked under his arm, he spoke gently to the golden bird. "Friend, you were born to soar. It is better that you die here today on the rocks below than live the rest of your life being a chicken in a pen, gawked at and out of your element." Having said these final words, he lifted the eagle up and once more commanded it to "FLY!" He tossed it out into the open space and this time, much to his relief, it opened its seven-foot wingspan and flew gracefully into the sky. It slowly climbed in ever higher spirals, riding unseen thermals of hot air until it disappeared into the glare of the morning sun.

You may have been brought up in an environment that limited your understanding of your potential. You may have grew up among folks that were content with their comfort zones, have no vision of greatness and never imagined anything significant. It's never too late to unlock your potential. It's never too late to spread your wings like that beautiful eagle that was stuck in the farmer's chicken coop. If you believe in yourself you can fly and soar like the eagle. You might as well start singing the song *"I believe I Can Fly"* by R Kelly to yourself.

You may think your life is awful, but if you can believe in yourself, you will unlock your God-given potential and ability. You will spread your wings and fly away to the limitless space of high achievements and great accomplishments.

Comfort Zone

Comfort Zone! Sounds familiar? We all have our comfort zones. These can be activities, situations, routines or places that we feel comfortable, safe and secure. We enjoy our comfort zone as they are usually easy, familiar, predictable, and comforting and with little or no risk at all. That's why most people live in their comfort zones all their life. The problem with being in a comfort zone is that it breeds complacency and limits potential.

I read an article on the website of Manage Train Learn, one of the UK's premier training companies, about the need to overcome our natural instinct to play safe and develop our talents, strengths and potential so that we can be all we can be. There are profound truths and insights in the article. Here are some extracts from the article:

"There are two pulls in the human condition: the pull to stay where we are and consolidate what we have; and the pull to discover what is still possible, what we could achieve, how far we could go. The result of these two opposing pulls is that some of us - perhaps the majority - choose the path of safety and security while wondering what we might have missed. Others take risks, go on adventures, seek to maximise what they possess, even at the expense of a quiet life. That's why, while many people exist in a state of survival and maintenance, others adventure into states of growth and development.

"A state of surviving is about living from day to day, managing to get by, keeping our heads above water.

"The state of 'maintenance' is one most people are in for much of their lives. It is a safe balance between ourselves and our environment which occasionally may go against us if we are unlucky, or in our favour if we are lucky. Maintenance is the steady job, the money in the bank for a rainy day, the relationship which is fine but based on routine and security. Maintenance is like being on a surfboard on the open seas. We can thank God that we're not in the water floundering around;

most of our efforts are focused on staying upright and not falling off. Yet, as we sail along, without any other aim than to stay upright, there is the nagging feeling that perhaps there is more to life than just drifting along aimlessly.

"The state of development is of a different order to that of survival and maintenance. Whereas these are ways of coping with our environments, development is a state which we control and determine ourselves. We move from survival and maintenance into development when we decide that our lives will be qualitatively better than now, that we will use our inner gifts and strengths and that we will move to new goals and achievements."

Friend, I don't know which state you are in your life right now, but you can make a choice where you want to be. I can guarantee you that choosing to stay in your comfort zone is a choice to be less than what God has created you to be. Why be less when you can be all that God had created you to be? Why settle for little when you can accomplish much more? Why stay in your comfort zone when you can venture into a state of growth and development? Only you can answer the questions, but you need to answer them honestly and frankly if you really want to unlock and maximise your potential. A word of caution: when answering the questions, no excuses!

Excuses

There was a popular convenience store in the town where I grew up as a teenager. In front of the store was a big bold sign that read "No excuses". The sign was visible to both customers and passer-by, and many people in the town associated the store with the sign. I remember I used to say to my friends then, "Let's go for shopping at no excuses". Growing up, I figured out that the store owner was smart enough to pre-empt the human tendency to give excuses for not wanting to pay for items purchased, or asking for credit. This seems logical since it was a community town, and almost everyone knew each other. Some of the customers were friends, families and neighbours of the store owner.

Excuses are simply rationalisation we make to avoid responsibility. They are easy to come up with;

"I am very busy"
"There is no time"
"I don't have enough money"
"If I was born in a different country"
"It's because I could not get help"
"If my parents were rich"
"I am still young"
"It's too late for me"
"I am too old"

Excuses allow many people to stay in their comfort zone. I have met talented people with great potential held hostage by excuses as to why they couldn't do things they ought to and were able to do. They allowed their fears, insecurities, negative experiences and past failures to put them in an underserved jail. People who habitually give excuses are limiting their own potential and being unfair to themselves.

In John Chapter 5, the Bible tells a story about a man who Jesus healed by a pool in Jerusalem. The pool was called Bethesda. Before Jesus came to the pool, an angel would visit this pool during a certain season and stirred the water. Whoever stepped into the bubbling water was healed of whatever illness or infirmity he or she had. Many people flocked by the multitudes to this pool to be healed. Some of them were blind, impotent or crippled. These people would wait desperately by the pool for the angel to stir the water;

however, not everyone received their healing. When Jesus came to the pool, he saw a man who had been lame for 38 years. When Jesus learned that he had been in this condition for a long time, he asked him, "Do you want to be well?"

Rather than answering the direct question asked by Jesus about whether or not he really wants to get well, the man responded with excuses about why he was not able to get into the pool to try to be healed. He replied "I have no one to help me into the pool when the water is stirred, while I am trying to get in, someone goes ahead of me." Jesus told the man to get up, pick up his bed and walk. The man instantly became well when he stepped out in faith, inspired by the power of the words spoken by Jesus.

Friend, no more excuses! When you make excuses, you postpone your opportunities. Many times, you have to encourage and motivate yourself. You have to stir those desires in your heart and say to the Lord, "Yes, I really want it!" rather than make excuses.

Comparison

One of the most common and disruptive hindrances to human potential is comparison. Parents compare their children to each other. Some compare their child with that of friends, cousins, and classmates. Some teachers compare pupils with their peers and siblings.

"Jimmy is smarter than you"
"Jonny is not as proactive as Jimmy"
"Why can't you be like your brother?"
"Why can't you get the same grade as your friend?"

Parents who compare their child unfavourably with others feel the need to shape their child according to their desires and ideals rather than helping the child identify his or her talents or interests. Children have different talents, abilities, interests and personalities. Every child is different and unique. Each child's strength may be completely different to that of his siblings and peers. Comparison affects a child's self-esteem. A child who is continually subjected to unfavourable comparison with others over time will accept that he is not good enough and will start acting and make choices based on his low esteem.

Peter J Daniel's potential was almost destroyed by his teacher Miss Phillips. Having been branded 'stupid' by Miss Phillips and told he would never amount to anything in life at the age of 14, he left school and moved from one menial job to another. Dissatisfied about life he decided to be an apprentice bricklayer. Thanks to God who had put seeds of greatness in him. When Peter Daniel gave his life to Jesus, he started unlocking his God-given potential. Against all odds he transformed himself from being an illiterate bricklayer's assistant to a millionaire through real estate and other business interests around the world. He wrote many motivational books including a book "*Miss Phillip You Were Wrong*".

You'll be surprised just how long memories of comparison can stay in a child's mind - it can stay with him even when he becomes an adult.

When I was at high school, I found maths, physics and science challenging. I did not like maths and put little effort into it. However, I enjoyed literature, history, religious studies and economics. Oh I loved reading story books especially William Shakespeare books, *The Canterbury Tales* by Geoffrey Chaucer and other literature books. My younger brother on the other hand was very good in maths and other science subjects. He is now a pharmacist. One of our older relatives used to compare my performance in science and in maths with my brother's performance. He came to our house a few days after we vacated for the end of the year session. He asked about our examination reports and my parents showed him our reports. After reading the reports, he summoned my brother and I to the living room, praised my brother for his performance, gave him some money for his good performance, especially maths. He then turned to me and said

"I will not give you any money because of your poor performance, even your brother is better than you in maths." I felt miserable because of his remarks. It was an experience that haunted me for many years. Unfortunately my parents did not know better at that time. They were also caught up in the comparison trap. They wanted me to be a doctor, an engineer or an accountant. As I was under constant pressure to improve my performance in science and maths, I felt less than other students who performed better than me in maths and science. I thought they were geniuses and that I could not reach their level. I wrongly believed that only the geniuses on earth are scientists and inventors. I thank God that I now know better. I have learnt to appreciate my uniqueness and my areas of interest.

You are too unique to be compared with someone else. Your potential, gifts, talents and abilities are entirely unique to you, as is your purpose on earth. They can never be compared with anyone else.

I can imagine the humiliation, pain and rejection Jepththah suffered from his half-brothers because of the circumstances of his birth.

"We are better than you"

"You are an illegitimate child"

"You are not entitled to have an inheritance in our father's house"

"Your mother is a harlot"

Jephthah's half-brothers continued to oppress him until he could no longer bear the abuse. He fled from his father's house and became homeless.

In Judges 11:3 we see that *"Jephthah fled from his brothers and settled in the land of Tob. Soon he had a gang of scoundrels gathered around him and following him"*. This group of people were described as worthless and they lacked identity and sense of direction. Jephthah became their leader and this caused him to start unlocking his potential. He was courageous, brave, and focused. Jephthah must have learnt despite his rejection by his family that God loved him and that he was important to God. God was not looking at the circumstances of his birth. Before Jephthah was born God had great plans for him and put in him leadership and warring ability. He was ordained to be a leader, deliverer and a judge. No wonder years after he fled his family, when elders of Gilead sought his help to defend the nation against the enemy's attack, he gave them a condition: that he would fight for them and if he were to win he would be their new leader. And God backed him up by granting him victory over the enemy. Jephthah led Israel to victory and he became the judge in Israel.

Friend, don't allow how others treat you or their opinion of you take away your self-worth. You are precious and worth more than gold in the sight of God.

In 2 Corinthians 10:12, the Bible states that those who measure themselves by themselves, or compare themselves among themselves are not wise. You may never unlock or maximise your God-given potential if you continue to compare yourself with others or try to be someone else.

Attitude

It is often said that "your attitude will determine your altitude". Your attitude can either help you unlock your potential or hold you back. People with negative attitudes see impossibilities, magnify problems, expect defeats, do nothing, achieve nothing, become nothing, and wallow in self-pity.

The account of the report of the twelve spies in the Bible in Numbers Chapter 13 is illustrative of impact of attitude, both negative and positive.

When the Israelites arrived at the border of Canaan, Moses selected twelve men - one man from each of the tribes of Israel - and sent them to investigate the land that God promised for their inheritance. He told them to go into the land and bring back information about the people and their cities. He also told them to bring back some of the fruit that was growing in the land. The men went into the land and were there for forty days. They found that it was a really good land. When they returned to the camp, they showed Moses and Israelites the good fruits they had found in the land. The grapes were so big that it took two men to carry a cluster on a pole between them. Ten of the men reported "It is really a land flowing with milk and honey. But the inhabitants of the land are Giants, big and powerful and the cities are large with high walls around them". They concluded in their report, "The land we explored is one that devours those who live there. We can't attack the people! They are too strong for us. All the people we saw are very tall. We felt as small as grasshopper, and that's how we must have looked to them." The other two men, Joshua and Caleb, however gave a different report. They said to Moses and the whole congregation "Let us go up at once and possess the land, for we are able to overcome it".

The report of the ten spies caused confusion, fear, doubt and rebellion in the Israelites' camp. The people were afraid when they heard the reports, they turned against Moses the leader, criticised him, and were ready to select a new leader to lead them back to Egypt. They were willing to go back into bondage instead of moving forward in faith and courage to possess the Promised Land! Despite the persuasion of Joshua and Caleb, the people were tearful, discouraged and refused to proceed in their journey. They could not go on to take the Canaan land at that time. Obviously, God was not pleased with the Israelites and the negative report given by the ten spies. God punished them by making them wander in the wilderness for forty years. God determined that they would wander in the wilderness one year for each day the spies were spying out the land. So for forty years the Israelites wandered in the wilderness. Of all the adults who were twenty years or older at the time the Israelites left Egypt, only Joshua and Caleb entered the Promised Land. Their positive attitude granted them grace and favour of the Lord. The rest of the adults died in the wilderness because of their negative attitude.

In Numbers 13:32, the Bible described the report of the ten spies as an 'evil report'. The report revealed the attitude of the ten men. They were negative, fearful, suffered from an inferiority complex and lacked faith. They did not trust that God who promised them the land was able to help them overcome the giants and the other obstacles in the land. They held on to their negative report despite the intervention of Joshua and Caleb. Their report and actions revealed deeper attitude problems of a critical spirit, ingratitude, unbelief and rebellion to God's delegated authority. It is sad to know that their attitude hindered them at that defining moment of their journey to the Promised Land. They missed their opportunity and they never had another one.

The report given by Joshua and Caleb was one of hope and optimism. Their vision of God and experience of God overshadowed the size of the giants and any obstacles that might have confronted them. They envisioned possibilities instead of impossibilities. They were positive, courageous, and strong in the Lord. They saw themselves as mighty men. They trusted God fully and expected victory and not defeat. They were fully persuaded, without any doubt, that with God on their side they were well able to possess the land. And so they did forty years later! No wonder God testified about them, saying that they had 'a different spirit'. Theirs was a positive attitude.

There is an old story about two salesmen who demonstrated different attitudes to similar situations. Many years ago, two salesmen were sent by a British shoe manufacturer to Africa to investigate and report back on the market potential. The first salesman reported back "There is no potential here - nobody wears shoes". The second reported, "There is massive potential here - nobody wears shoes".

This short story illustrates how people can view the same situation but interpret it differently. Some people see situations in terms of their problems, difficulties, disadvantages, obstacles and impossibilities, whereas others may instead see opportunities, possibilities and potential solutions to problems.

I have come to realise that the most important decision we make each day is the attitude we choose to embrace. Our attitudes are subjective, based on how we perceive our world, situations and circumstances. For example, you might wake up one morning and find that you're in pain or experiencing some level of discomfort. You can choose to tell yourself, "This pain will go away, I must get out of bed". Usually the pain leaves the moment you rise up to have a shower or engage in some form of activity to kickstart your day. On the other hand, you may allow a negative attitude to sabotage your day by telling yourself, "This pain is too much. I can't get out of bed, I need some more sleep". The Bible addresses such a negative attitude in Proverbs 6 this way, *"How long will you lie there, you sluggard? When will you get up from your sleep? A little sleep, a little slumber, a little folding of the hands to rest and poverty will come on you like a thief, and scarcity like an armed man"* (vs 9-11 NIV). In other words, wake up! Change your attitude! A lazy attitude will hinder your effectiveness. As the popular idiom goes "A word to the wise is sufficient". It appears my interpretation is too lenient for some people. I charge you to examine your life by meditating on Proverbs 6: 6-11.

In order to unlock your potential, you need a positive 'can-do attitude', like that demonstrated by Joshua and Caleb, and by the second salesman who saw a new opportunity. I don't know what kind of attitude you have, be it positive or negative? The good news is that you can change your attitude from negative to positive. No one can change your attitude for you. It's got to be you. I believe we all need to undergo regular attitude checks. Simply put, you need to regularly examine your attitude just as car owners in the UK are required by law to take their cars for an MOT test. Some problems are obvious and easily identified by observation, while some are hidden and only detectable by honest scrutiny. You must be willing to face the truth and admit to yourself areas of your attitude that are negative and you must be willing to make the necessary adjustments. It does cost a little of our ego to fix our negative attitudes, but the price is worth it when we experience the joy, peace and power of a changed life.

I remember in 2003, I had to examine my attitude by asking myself sincere and objective questions. That true and honest attitude check set me free from the yoke of bitterness. I was free to unlock (and continually develop) my God-given potential. Since then, I try to constantly examine myself in different areas of my life. I must admit, I am not yet perfect. As Apostle Paul states in Philippians 3:12 *"I don't mean to say that I have already achieved these things or that I have already reached perfection. But I press on to possess that perfection for which Christ Jesus first possessed."*

How to Maximise Your Potential

In order to maximise your potential, you first have to recognise it. You must identify your God-given gift, skill, talent or ability. I often hear people talk about reaching their potential. Really, your potential is not something you strive to reach. It's already within you, waiting to be discovered.

Do you know your potential? Do you recognise the unique gifts, talents and abilities that your Creator has put in you? Are you making use of them? If you have not yet discovered your potential, here are some clues that can help you recognise or discover your gifts, skills, talents and abilities. Look within and ask yourself the following questions:

➢ What are the things you love to do?

➢ What ignites your curiosity?

➢ What do you have passion for?

Bill Gates, the founder of Microsoft (the world's largest PC software company), started showing interest in computer programming at the of 13 when he was at Lakeside school, a private independent school in Seattle, Washington. In his eighth grade, he became fascinated with what computers could do. His school had just acquired a computer terminal and at that time, Computer Centre Corporation, a local firm offered to provide computer time for students. Young Bill Gates was fascinated by the machine and how it would always execute software code perfectly. Throughout high school, he and his future business partner, Paul Allen, took every opportunity to explore the potential uses of this new technology, and taught themselves basic computer programming.

Bill Gates graduated from Lakeside School in 1973 and enrolled at Harvard University to pursue law, following his parents' wishes, although his true love was for computers. He soon changed course and worked his way through the University's upper level maths and computer science classes. He spent more time in the computer labs than in class. He stayed up all night marvelling at the wonders of what a computer could do. Eventually, he dropped out of Harvard in 1976 to found Microsoft with Paul Allen. Microsoft released Windows in 1985 and went public in 1986. By 1987, Bill Gates was a billionaire.

Friend, what you love doing can be a clue to your potential and God-given gift. Steve Jobs, Apple's founder, once said "You've got to find what you love. If you haven't found it yet, keep looking. Don't settle. As with all matters of the heart, you'll know when you've found it."

Tiger Woods, an American professional golfer and one of the most successful golfers of all time, enjoys playing golf. He once said "I love to play golf, and that's my arena. And you can characterise it and describe it however, you want, but I have a love and passion for getting the ball in the hole and beating those guys". He has a passion for golf. He is addicted to playing golf!

People who love what they do are passionate about it. They enjoy what they do. They are excited about whatever they are doing and are willing to get up early or stay up late to work on it. The time is now 2.00am on Saturday 11th July 2015. I have been alone in the sitting room for over three hours writing. My wife and boys have been in bed since around 10.00pm. I had a nap between 7.00pm to 9.00pm, had a shower, and then came downstairs to write. I enjoy what I am doing. I am passionate about this book. Thinking of the inspiration, encouragement and empowerment that this book will give you gives me an unceasing drive, energy and joy. I love it. I am excited and will gladly spend the rest of my life working on activities and projects that will inspire and help people unlock and maximise their unique potentials.

➤   What are the problems you love to solve for others? The problems you are willing to solve for others can also provide clues to your potential.

Although Florence Nightingale was born into a rich and upper class British family, as a young woman she devoted her life to the service of others. Despite her family's opposition to her working as a nurse, she worked hard to educate herself in the art and science of nursing. She believed nursing was her calling. Her passion and desire to serve led her to the Crimean War of 1854.

In late 1854, the Secretary of War, Sidney Herbert, designated Florence Nightingale to organise a corps of nurses to the Military Hospital in Scutari, Turkey, to tend to the sick and fallen soldiers. Florence assembled a team of 34 nurses and sailed to Crimea. She was horrified by the poor condition of the hospital barrack when she arrived in Constantinople. The hospital sat on the top of a large cesspool which contaminated the water that soldiers were drinking. The hospital barrack was filthy, the floor was filled with faeces, many wounded soldiers were laid on their own excrement on stretchers. More soldiers were dying of infectious diseases, such as typhoid and cholera, caused by the terrible living conditions, than the injuries incurred in the battle!

Florence and her team of nurses went into action. They cleaned the hospital and ensured the wounded soldiers were well-fed and clothed. Florence spent every minute caring for the soldiers and in the evening she moved through the dark hallways carrying a lamp and making rounds, ministering to the wounded soldiers. Her compassion earned her the name "The lady with the lamp" among some of the soldiers. She also created a number of patient services which contributed to improving the quality of life in the hospital, such as laundry services, a classroom and a library.

After her service in the War, she wrote an 800-page report analysing her observations on matters affecting the health and efficacy of the British army, as well as a proposal for reformation in other military hospitals operating under poor conditions. Her report not only demonstrated her passion for reformation, her use of relevant graphs and statistics showed professional competence, good record-keeping and the ability to present information in a clear and concise manner. Her report influenced the restructuring of the War Office's Administration Department, including establishment of a Royal Commission for Heath of the British Arm in 1857. Her knowledge and experience also helped lay a foundation for improvement in the field of nursing and care.

Florence was a catalyst of change. Her willingness to serve others unlocked her compassion, professional competence, presentation skills, leadership and ability to influence.

Jesus, often moved by compassion, loved to solve problems for people. He recognised the grace and anointing of God upon His life to solve spiritual, emotional, mental and health problems for people. His compassion for the sick, oppressed, and spiritually blind unlocked the gifts of God within Him. At the beginning of His earthly ministry, He clearly identified His potential, God-given gifts, mission, as well as the beneficiaries of the grace of God upon His life. No wonder He boldly declared *'The Spirit of the Lord is on me, because he has anointed me to proclaim good news to the poor. He has sent me to proclaim freedom for the prisoners and recovery of sight for the blind, to set the oppressed free"* (Luke 4:18 NIV). He devoted His life to using the anointing and grace of God upon His life to solve problems for humanity.

After His resurrection and ascension into heaven, Peter - one of His disciples - testified about the love and power of God upon his life. He stated in Acts 10:38 *"God anointed Jesus of Nazareth with the Holy Spirit and with power, who went about doing good, and healing all that were oppressed of the devil; for God was with Him"* (NKJV). The problems that Jesus solved for people were indications of the anointing, compassion and gifts of the Holy Spirit upon His life.

Have you clearly identified the problem or problems you feel the need to solve for people? This may be an indication of the unique gifts, abilities and capabilities within you. Don't ignore the problems around you, they can be gateways to unleash the hidden potential within you.

In Genesis 40, the Bible records that Joseph observed the sad countenance of King Pharaoh's chief butler and chief baker who were locked up in prison with him. He asked them "Why do you look so sad today?" They told him they had no one to interpret their dreams. Joseph was willing to help them solve their puzzle. This was a clear indication of his divine ability to interpret dreams, which eventually earned him favour before King Pharaoh.

I had a dream some years back. In the dream, I saw airplanes moving on a main road in a city. I also saw motorcars, trucks and motorcycles moving on the same road. Although I did not count the number of planes, however, I noted there were as many planes as were motorcars moving on the road. I also observed that planes, motorcars and motorcycles were overtaking one another as motorcars and motorcycles would normally overtake other vehicles on the road. It appeared the airplanes were conditioned to move on the main road as if they were created for roads. As I observed the planes, I started wondering, why are these planes moving on the road? Aren't they meant to be flying in the sky? I knew that planes are created to fly in the air, but why are these planes limited to the ground? I thought something was wrong, these planes are definitely not supposed to be on the ground!

When I woke up in the morning, I started wondering what the dream could mean. A few hours later, the Holy Spirit spoke to my heart that the planes I saw in my dream represent people who are gifted with great potentials and abilities, but operating below their capabilities. They are meant to be flying, but instead they are walking on the ground. They are created and endowed by their creator to accomplish great things but they are ignorant. They are doing less, expecting less, experiencing less than is possible and are contented with their status quo. I thought about the statement of King Solomon in Ecclesiastes 10:7 *"Princes are walking as servants upon the earth"*.

Inspired by this dream, I felt that I need to help as many people as possible to unlock and maximise their God-given potential. I started seeing the unique gifts and abilities that God has deposited in me to inspire, encourage, motivate and challenge people to unlock and maximise their potential. Moved with compassion and purpose, I wrote down my personal statement of purpose as "Inspiring, encouraging and challenging people to recognise, develop, activate and maximise their natural and God-given potential, gifts, talents and abilities."

Looking back in my life, I realised how much God has helped me to move from a law profession to develop a career as a preacher, pastor, writer and life coach. I clearly understood that a career in law was not for me. I recognised that God had called and gifted me to solve different problems for people that are not necessarily legal. No wonder I did not have real passion for law as a student in the university. Like Bill Gates, I decided to study law, following my parents' wishes of seeing their son in a prestigious and lucrative profession! It took me a 14 Year journey of inner search, walking with God, and persistence to discover and unlock my hidden potential. This has now moved me into the arenas of preaching, pastoring, writing, motivating, coaching, and helping people fulfil their dreams and destinies.

Please don't get me wrong, I am not blaming my parents for their initial influence on my career choice. I appreciate their sacrifice and the value of education they have given me as a young boy. As JK Rowling, stated in her commencement address at the Annual meeting of Harvard Association, "There is an expiry date on blaming your parents for steering you in the wrong direction; the moment you are old enough to take the wheel, responsibility lies with you". That is exactly what I did. I am now the driver of my own life and destiny. Are you? You better be! However, you need God by your side to lead and guide you in the right way.

Are you willing to be a problem solver? The problems you are willing to solve for others may be the vital key to unlocking your potential. Maybe you are already solving problems for others and still not sure about your potential. Don't give up! The Lord will shine his light upon any darkness in your life.

I feel compelled to offer you wise counsel. You cannot solve every problem for everyone. Indeed you do not have the ability to solve everyone's problems. Your unique gifts and abilities have been given to solve a specific problem or problems for specific reasons, probably at specific times. Don't overburden yourselves with trying to solve everyone's problems. Any attempt to solve everyone's problems or any problem thrown at you can drain you of energy and purpose.

There is an old story about a lighthouse keeper who worked on a rocky stretch of coastline. Once a month he would receive a new supply of oil to keep the light burning so that ships could safely sail near the rocky coast. One night, a woman from a nearby village came and begged him for some oil to keep her family warm. Another time a father asked for some to use in his lamp. Another man needed to lubricate a wheel. All the requests seemed legitimate; the lighthouse keeper tried to please everyone and so he granted all their requests.

Towards the end of the month, he noticed his supply of oil was very low. Soon it was gone and one night the light on the lighthouse went out. As a result, that evening several ships were wrecked and countless lives were lost. When the authorities investigated, the man was very apologetic. He told them he was just trying to be helpful with the oil. Their reply to his excuses, however, was simple and to the point: "You were given oil for one purpose, and one purpose only - to keep that light burning!" I pray the Lord grant you wisdom and discernment to know the problems you are empowered by God to solve.

➤ What are the things that come naturally to you?

Another clue that can help you unlock your potential is by considering things that come naturally to you. They may be where your strength and potential lie.

Think of things that you do effortlessly. For some people it's teaching, accounting, selling and marketing, computing, repairing and fixing things. Some people are great inventors, while others are great scientists. Some people are naturally caring and compassionate. They love caring for people, empathising, encouraging others, working with children or providing care to the elderly or the sick. Usually the things that come naturally to you will also be things you enjoy doing, though they may still require time and effort on your part to improve on them. Think of the things you do well, probably better than others. It could even be areas others have noticed and commended you for. Everyone has things that come naturally to us, while we struggle in other areas. We all have things that we do easily or effortlessly that others may struggle with. Some people are gifted speakers while others are great entertainers or sportsmen.

I hope you will consider the questions and clues I have shared with you carefully. Taking the time to think carefully and answer the questions can unveil your potential and set you on an adventure of personal fulfilment and significance.

Once you have discovered your potential or become aware of your natural gifts or abilities, you have the responsibility to develop them. The best way to develop your gifts is by using them. You must be willing to take the time and effort necessary to develop your abilities to their fullest capacities. The more you use your gifts and talents, the more proficient you become. As it is often said 'practice makes perfect'. To improve incrementally, you must use your potential.

Michael Johnson stunned the world in the 1996 Olympics in Atlanta, Georgia, USA, when he achieved what no other sprinter had ever accomplished. He won two gold medals, for the 200 metres and 400 metres, in the same Olympics. His 200-metre time of 19.32 seconds stood as the world record for 12 years. He currently holds the World and Olympics record for 400 metres, a feat he accomplished with a time of 43.18 seconds at the 1999 World Athletics Championships events in Seville, Spain. His stiff upright running stance and very short steps defied the conventional wisdom that a high knee lift was essential for maximum speed. Michael Johnson is generally considered as one of the greatest and most consistent sprinters in the history of track and field athletics.

Like many successful and great achievers, Michael Johnson did not reach his peak performance overnight. It took over a decade of hard work, consistent training, goal setting, competitions, victories and losses to maximise his talent. He started running competitively at age 10, winning a blue ribbon as the fastest in a 50-

yard dash at a local mini Olympics organised for young talented kids. In his high school, he was one of the top 200 metre sprinters and continued maximising his potential when he was studying as a undergraduate at Baylor University in Waco, Texas. At the university, his coach, Clyde Hart initially chose him to be part of the relay team. It was not long before that Clyde saw greater potential in him. Michael broke the university record for 200 metres in his first race with a time of 20.41 seconds. After graduating from the university in 1990 with a Bachelor degree in Accounting and Marketing, he started running track professionally. In 1991, at world championships events in Tokyo, he won his first world title in 200 metres and won the world title in both 400 metres and 4 x 400 metres relay. Throughout his professional career, he has ran 200 metres in less than 20 seconds 23 times, and has ran 400 metre races in under 44 seconds 22 times. Since retiring from competitive track in 2008, he has been working as a sports commentator - regularly appearing on BBC - where he offers his expert views during coverage of athletic events. He has truly maximised his potential.

You may not be a sprinter like Michael Johnson, but you can achieve significant improvement in your area of gifting and talent. Everyone has specific areas of talents and abilities that can be maximised to utmost peak performance. You must be willing to commit to hard work, practice, discipline and determination to bring the best out of yourself. John Maxwell in his book *'Beyond Talent'* states "If you want to sum up what lifts most successful individuals above the crowd, you could do it with four little words: a little bit more." He is absolutely right. A little bit more practice, a bit more practice, a bit more practice. You cannot overdo practice. Consistent and purposeful practice will enable you to hone your talent or craft, whatever it is. That's how you maximise your potential to its fullest.

Kobe Bryant of the Los Angeles Lakers is one of the most successful basketball players of all time. His talent flourished early in high school when he made a record to be the topmost basketball player of the nation in high school. He started playing for the NBA as soon as he finished high school and went on to win 5 NBA Championships and 2 Olympic Gold Medals. He is a 17-time All-Star, 15-time member of the All-NBA Team, and ranks third on both the league's all-time regular season scoring. He is one of the highest scorers in the league averaging almost 26 points per games. He was also the youngest player in NBA history to reach 30,000 career points. Kobe's outstanding career achievements can only be matched by a few superstars.

Obviously Kobe did not reach these heights on a platter of gold. He trains harder and longer than anyone else in the NBA. He devotes 6 hours a day to regular exercises 6 times a week. His 6-hour workout features a hefty mix of track work, basketball skills improvements and weightlifting. He normally makes 700 to 1,000 shots a day! Consistent and purposeful practice is the secret of his game. Of course, Kobe understands the value of rest. He schedules one day a week for relaxation.

Are you willing to commit to consistent practice in order to maximise your potential? Are you willing to push yourself beyond limits? Are you willing to pay the price of consistent and purpose driven practice? It's all about choice.

Are you ready to go? Wait a minute, don't go for big goals. Start with small goals. You must be willing to take baby steps in order to maximise your potential. Set small manageable goals that can help you towards your ultimate purpose. For example you might be thinking of running a marathon one day. First, set goals of walking for about 15 minutes a day, then increase it to 30 minutes, and then try jogging for 30 minutes a day.

As Daniel Coyle states in his book '*The Little Book of Talent*', "You aren't built to be transformed in a single day. You are built to improve little by little, connection by connection, rep by rep". That's the secret to all improvements.

Another secret to continuous improvement that you have to embrace in order to maximise your potential is commitment to lifelong learning. You must be willing to learn from your successes, your achievements, your failures, and your mistakes. You can also learn from other people, their successes, lifestyles, work ethics, and habits. There is wide range of gold mines to learn from throughout your lifetime. Really you cannot learn enough. You will always have the opportunity to learn as long as you are willing to learn. As great a player as he is, Kobe Bryant is always hungry for more. Certainly not for more junk food, but more exploits in his craft. He takes time to watch the playback of all his games with his coach, analysing his performance in order to see how he may improve. A few days ago I watched one of his interviews with sportscaster Ahmad Rashad, aired by NBA TV, on YouTube. In response to a question from Ahmad about how he feels now that he had got something that makes him bigger and better, Kobe responded "I want more, I want to learn more. How can I learn more, I want to learn these things more, there has got to be another level". Friend, are you willing to learn more? Are you willing to commit to continuous improvements? Blessed are you if you are still hungry and thirsty for insights, knowledge, wisdom and understanding, improvements, skills developments and experience. You will surely maximise your potential to its fullest.

Chapter Five

Speak Faith-Filled Words

Many years ago, one of my brothers had an accident while playing football at school. He was in secondary school at the time. During the match, one of the opponents kicked him in the nose. His nose was badly injured. However, he did not report the accident to any of the teachers at school, nor tell my parents when he got home. He kept it to himself for a few days, suffering in silence. By the third day, he could no longer endure the agony. By this time his nose was swollen and bleeding. He had no choice but to tell my parents who immediately rushed him to the hospital.

An X-ray revealed that his nose was fractured and he needed to undergo surgery immediately. A few hours before the operation, one of the consultants had a pre-surgery meeting with my parents to discuss the procedure and the possible side effects with them. During the meeting, the consultant advised my parents that due to the severity of the injury my brother would have a saddle nose. My mother immediately responded. "Doctor, my son will not have a saddle nose. I reject that. My son's nose will be perfect." The doctor tried to explain to my mother that it was almost impossible for my brother to have a nose that was not deformed after the operation, but my mother kept on affirming her conviction that her son would have a perfect nose.

After the procedure, the lead consultant informed my parents that the operation had gone well. Gradually the nose healed. Despite the false alarm raised by the doctor, my brother did not have a saddle nose or any deformity. Thanks to the faith-filled words spoken by my mother before the operation. Although the doctor was speaking based on his experience and knowledge, my mother was speaking a different language based on her conviction and knowledge of God. Her words were filled with faith and life. They were not empty words. I believe God honoured my mother's positive confession and overrode the doctor's report and granted my brother a perfect healing.

The Power of Words

Your words hold incredible power, both positively and negatively. Your words can bring victory or defeat. They can build up or tear down. The Bible in Proverbs 18:21 put it this way, *"Death and life are in the power of the tongue, and those who love it will eat its fruit."*

Whatever you think about and say aloud has the ability to affect your life and the lives of those around you. That's why you should learn to speak words of faith instead of speaking negative words.

I am intrigued by the faith and trust expressed by Abraham when he was tested by God according to the scriptures in Genesis 22. God gave Abraham a strong command, though it was a test to see if Abraham loved his son Isaac more than he loved God. God told him to offer Isaac as a burnt offering to Him on a mountain called Moriah. The command was hard for Abraham because he loved his son Isaac very much. Moreso, he had waited so long for the miraculous birth of Isaac. However, he had learned to trust God even when he did not understand. So he planned to obey God. He told

Isaac that they were going to offer a sacrifice to God, but he did to tell him of his plan to offer him as the burnt offering. As they set out, Isaac carried the wood while Abraham carried the fire and knife. On their way, Isaac observed that they did not have with them the lamb they would need to offer the sacrifice, so he innocently asked his father "Where is the lamb for the burnt offering?" Abraham simply replied "God Himself will provide the lamb."

When they got to the place where God instructed him to offer the sacrifice, while he was preparing to offer his son as sacrifice, God immediately shouted to Abraham through an angel and instructed him to stop and never sacrifice his son. He had passed the test. God was impressed that Abraham did not withhold Isaac from Him and so he did not need to offer his son as a sacrifice. Instead God opened his eyes to see a ram in the nearby bushes. He offered the ram as a sacrifice instead of his son. I am sure that Isaac would have thought that God did provide just as father said. In the midst of trial, Abraham spoke words filled with faith and trust in God. His faith-filled words attracted divine provisions of the lamb used for the sacrifice.

What are your words producing in your life today? Are they producing the fruits you desire or are they producing undesirable fruits? Are your words attracting provisions into your life or moving divine provisions and miracles out of your reach?

There was a great famine in Samaria. This story is recorded in the Bible in 2 Kings Chapters 6 and 7. Syria, the enemy of Samaria, had besieged the city with the whole army. The Samarians were so afraid about the enemy's attack that no one could enter or go out of the city. This resulted in a shortage of food and other essential amenities in the city. The people of Samaria were in great distress. The famine was so severe at that time that a donkey's head sold for eighty shekels of silver and a half pint of dove manure for five shekels of silver. People were even eating their own children. The King was very disturbed about their predicament, but he had no answer to the curse and distress in the city.

Though the King blamed God for the calamity that came upon Israel and Samaria, God still had a word and solution to their national problem. God promised through Prophet Elisha that in 24 hours, the economic situation in Samaria would be such abundance that the food prices would radically drop. What a great promise! However, one of the king's officers mocked this prophecy, saying, "Even if God would make windows in the heaven could such a thing happen?" However, Elisha the prophet replied "You will see it with your eyes, but you will not benefit from it."

God has a way of fulfilling His words and promises. He can use any situation, circumstance, and people to bring His Word to pass. He can even use the most unusual situation and least expected people to bring His Word to pass.

There were four lepers outside the city gates. The four lepers were hungry. They had lost hope of getting any food from the city. If they stayed outside the city walls, they would perish. If they went to the camp of the Syrians, the Syrians might kill them or have mercy on them and spare their lives. They had a decision to make. They decided to go outside the camp. By the time the lepers got to the camp of the Syrians, the Lord had caused the Syrians army to hear the sound like the sound of an invading army coming to their camp. They became panic-stricken and fled, leaving their tents and all their food supplies behind.

When the lepers entered the camp they found an abundance of food and other valuables. They ate and drank and helped themselves to a lot of valuables. For a while they feasted, and then they realised there was an abundance of food in the abandoned camp for all the city of Samaria. Right away the lepers wanted to share the good news with the whole city. The news they had was too good to keep. They went and reported it to the people in Samaria. The people looted the camp of the Syrians and, sure enough, the prophesy given by Elisha the prophet came to pass within 24 hours.

The officer who mocked the prophecy was assigned duty to keep the gate in Samaria. At the time of the mad rush of people who were going to and from the camp of Syrians to get food, he was knocked down, trodden upon and killed by the people in their haste for food. As Elisha said, he saw the prophecy come true, but he did not live long enough to enjoy it himself. His unbelief and negativity kept him from partaking of the bounty that the rest of the city enjoyed.

Be careful with what you say and how you say it. Guard you mouth and avoid speaking anything that does not produce life. Too often when trials and tribulations come we give in to our doubts, fears and unbelief instead of declaring the words of faith.

"I just don't seem to be able to move ahead"
"Well, I have been praying for years without change"
"I can't be rich, I might as well stay poor"
"I can't make it"
"I'll never get well"
"I can't find a partner"
"This marriage can never work"
"This pain is killing me"

Some people say things like this about themselves when they are frustrated or when they make mistakes:

"I'm a fool"
"I am dull"
"I am stupid"

Friend, stop using words that line up with negative circumstances. Instead, line up your words with God's Word and release the power of His Word to work for you. Instead of speaking lack, defeats, and despair, start pronouncing God's blessing into your life.

"My God shall supply all my needs"
"The favour of God is upon my life"
"I am victorious"
"The Lord is my healer"
"My family is blessed"

When you declare God's Word and blessings upon your life, you are giving the angels of God permission to work and bring God's plans and purpose to pass in your life. In Psalm 103: 20-21, the Bible states that angels of God fulfil His Word and hearken to the voice of His Word. Do you realise that these very angels are waiting on the words of faith and hope to come out of your mouth? When you speak words of faith, you empower the angels to work on your behalf. In the book of James, Chapter 1, the Bible compared the human tongue to the rudder of a ship. Though the rudder is very small, it guides and directs the giant ship where to go. Your life is usually guided and directed by the words you speak. You can change the direction of your life by changing the words you speak.

Since 1993 when I was a young Christian, I knew I was called and anointed by God to preach and teach His Word to believers. I loved things of God and would spend hours in His presence praying and listening to God's Word. However, like Moses, I was initially focused on my inabilities instead of focusing on the abilities and power of God. I remember that the Senior Pastor of the church I used to attend asked me to be one of the leaders in the church. At another time, he wanted me to be the Pastor of a new church they were about to start overseas, but I excused myself by saying that I couldn't do it. The man of God told me that I was limiting myself by saying "I can't". It appeared that my use of "I can't" was almost self-fulfilled prophecy. For many years I could not venture into any significant leadership or pastoral work until I changed my words to "I can do anything that God had called me to do because His grace is sufficient for me". The course and direction of my life started to change dramatically when I started seeing myself in the light of God's calling on my life and speaking faith-filled words concerning my life and destiny.

In 1 Samuel 17, the Bible records the powerful words David spoke when he was about to confront Goliath. David said to the Philistine in verse 45, *"You come against me with sword and spear and javelin, but I come against you in the name of the Lord Almighty, the God of the armies of Israel, whom you have defied ... today I will give the carcasses of the Philistine army to the birds of the air and the whole world will know that there is a God in Israel it is not by sword or spear that the Lord saves; for the battle is the Lord's, and he will give all of you into our hands".* David's words were not empty words. They were filled with faith, power and life.

Backed by God, David moved in for the kill. He reached into his bag and slung one of his stones at Goliath's head. The stone sank into the giant's forehead and he fell face down on the ground. David then took Goliath's sword, killed him and then cut off his head. Surely your words can affect your action.

Your words can create your reality. When you speak words of hope, faith and optimism, you are using your words to create things that will appear in time. In the same way, if you continually speak words of despair, hopelessness and pessimism, you are also creating a reality, even though it may not be a desired reality. What you say is usually what you get!

Earlier on in this book, I told you the story of twelve spies as recorded in the Bible in Numbers 13. In their report, they stated *"We are not able to go up against the people (of Canaan), for they are too strong for us... The land is one that devours its inhabitants. And all the people that we saw in it are men of great stature. There we saw the Nephilim (the sons of Anaks are part of the Nephilim); and we were like grasshoppers in our own sight, and so we were in their sight.".* The report so discouraged Israel that the entire congregation raised a loud cry, and the people wept that night.

The report of the ten spies was bad, not because it lacked facts, but because it lacked faith. However, Caleb's words were different. According to the Bible he quiets the people and says, *"Let us go up at once and take possession of it; for we will certainly conquer it."* Unfortunately, the words of those ten spies created their realities. Of all the adults, twenty years and older, all but two died in the wilderness. Only two of the spies - Joshua and Caleb entered the Promised Land. Their faith-filled words also created their realities.

You too can create your desired realities by learning to speak faith-filled words, rather than magnifying your problems. Instead of aligning your words with your negative circumstances, fears and limitations, start pronouncing the blessings and promises of God upon your life and family. Pronounce the favour of God upon your life, family, situations, and circumstances rather than speaking your fears, doubts and unbelief.

In Mark 11:22-24, Jesus tells us that we can move mountains with faith-filled words. Your words, when accompanied with unwavering faith, can bring great results.

Speaking faith-filled words is God's way of bringing things into existence. The Bible reveals that God created the world in six days. He spoke His Word and everything came into existence.

Over and over in Genesis 1, we see the words, "And God said". Whatever God said became reality. He said, let there be light, let there be plants, let there be living creatures, and finally, let us make man in our own image. God's Word has the creative power to form, shape and design things exactly the way He wants.

No wonder God declares through one of His prophets in Isaiah 55:11, *"For as the rain and the snow come down from heaven, and do not return there without watering the earth and making it bear and sprout, and furnishing seed to the sower and bread to the eater: so will My word be which goes forth from My mouth; It will not return to Me empty, without accomplishing what I desire, and without succeeding in the matter for which I sent it."*

Every word spoken by God is backed up by faith. God operates by faith. He has confidence in His words. He believes in the integrity of His Word.

In Hebrews 11:3 the Bible states that

"Through faith we understand that the worlds were framed by the word of God, so that things which are seen were not made of things which do appear."

The Greek word translated "framed" in this scripture is "Katartizo". It means to fit together, render complete and perfect. The word also means to mend, repair and restore. Do you realise you were created in the image of God, after His likeness? You too can create your desired world by speaking faith-filled words.

Friend, you can frame, mend, repair or restore your life, family and environment by your words. May be you have experienced disappointments, frustration, failure and setbacks? Rather than seeing yourself as a failure, start declaring that:

"I am a winner"
"I am more than conqueror"
"I am born to reign"
"I am destined for greatness"
"I am valuable"
"I am the head and not the tail"
"My life is turning around for better"

Source of Faith

"A good man brings good things out of the good stored up in his heart, and an evil man brings evil things out of the evil stored up in his heart. For the mouth speaks what the heart is full of" (Luke 6:45).

Your mouth will speak what is in your heart. If your heart is filled with doubts, fears, negativity, bitterness and disappointments, these will be revealed through your words. If your heart is filled with hope, faith, confidence; it will manifest through your words. For your words to be filled with faith, you have to learn to fill your heart with faith. You may be wondering, how do I get faith?

In Romans 10:17, the Bible makes us to understand that *"Faith cometh by hearing, and hearing by the Word of God"*. The Word of God produces faith in your heart. Faith will develop in you when you cultivate the habit of hearing the Word of God.

Just as your body needs physical food for growth and nourishment, your spirit needs faith food for growth and strength. Without faith food, you will be weak spiritually and easily give in to defeat in times of adversity. One of the strategies of Satan is to make people speak contrary to God's plan and purpose for their lives. He usually brings adversity, trials and tribulations our way to try to weaken our faith and trust in God. He knows that words spoken out of doubts, unbelief, fear, bitterness and unforgiveness can cancel God's intended blessings and plans for His people.

When you fill your heart with the word of God on a consistent basis, you will build a reservoir of faith. Anytime you speak, faith and power will come out of your mouth. Friend, make a commitment to study and meditate on the Word of God on a consistent basis. You will be empowered to speak faith-filled words.

CHAPTER SIX

HAVE A BIG DREAM

Dr Martin Luther King was a Baptist preacher and civil rights leader in America. Although slavery was abolished following the civil war of 1861 to 1865, segregation remained in the southern states of America. Almost all aspects of life were segregated. African Americans were kept out of white schools, parks, theatres, hotels, swimming pools and restaurants. They had to sit in separate sections in trains and buses. As a young boy, Martin Luther experienced the racial discrimination of that time. When he was six years old, the parents of his white friends would not let him play with their children anymore.

In the midst of the segregation, Martin Luther had a dream, a big dream. A dream that sounded impossible to the world at that time. He had a strong desire that people in America would no longer be judged by the colour of their skin, that segregation would end, and that all men, women, and children could live as free human beings as created by God. In his speech 'I have a dream', Martin Luther declared his dream at the steps of the Lincoln Memorial in Washington DC in August 1963 to a crowd of over 250,000 people who were also demanding equal justice for all American citizens. In his own words, he declared "I have a dream that one day this nation will rise up and live out the true meaning of its creed: we hold truth to be self-evident that all men are created equal. I have a dream that my four little children will one day live in a nation where they will not be judged by the colour of their skin, but by the content of their character".

Tragically he was assassinated on April 4, 1968 while standing on the balcony of a motel in Memphis, Tennessee. Though the full manifestations of Martin Luther's dream were not fulfilled in his lifetime, his dream was fulfilled in the lifetime of his children and grandchildren. The election of President Barack Obama as the 44th President of America – making him the first black president in the history of America – is surely a fulfilment of his dream. When Barack Obama took the oath for his second term in office in January 2013, he placed his hand on two Bibles. The first was the Bible used by Abraham Lincoln, the 16th president of United States of America, and the second Bible, used by Dr Martin Luther King. What a great dream! Even though he died many years ago, his dream did not die. His dream prevailed against all adversity, occupied the White House and changed the history of America.

You have probably heard about Henry Ford, an American inventor engineer in the 20th century. Henry Ford had a great vision, a unique dream that would transform the automobile from a luxury that was only available to the rich, to a necessity for all. At that time, automobiles were expensive, custom-made machines which only the rich and affluent could afford. Henry Ford grew up in a farm owned by his parents, and might have easily become a farmer like his father, however, something stronger pulled at his imagination: the mechanics of machinery, and understanding how things worked. From an early age Ford loved to take things apart and put them back together again just to see how they worked. Neighbours and friends would bring him their broken watches to fix, thereby gaining a reputation as a watch repairer.

In June 1903, Henry Ford incorporated Ford Motor and proclaimed his dream "to create an inexpensive motorcar for the masses."

From 1908, the company began to produce Model T Cars. It was simple to drive, easy and cheap to repair. Model T was a huge success. Between 1908 and 1916, the sale price dropped from an initial offering of $825 to $360. It even dipped to as low as $280 within nineteen years of production. Nearly 15 million Model T cars were sold in the US alone. A car was no longer a luxury item for the rich; it became essential transportation for the ordinary man.

Model T irrevocably altered American society. As more Americans owned cars, urbanisation patterns changed. American soon became filled with cars, highways and gas stations. By the close of the 20th Century, Model T had received global recognition. The Model T was named the world most influential car of the 20th Century in an international poll. It was selected for the significant innovation it represented in its day, its design and its impact on both the auto industry and society itself. By his dream, Henry Ford transformed the automobile from an invention of unknown utility to an innovation that profoundly shaped the 20th Century. A dream is very powerful. It can change an individual, people, society, a nation, and the entire world.

The Power of Dreams

A dream is an idea conceived in your mind that you become passionate about. Your dream will set you apart from the rest of the people around you. I once read a quote that said "There are no great people, only great dreamers". Yes, your dream will bring you into greatness. Your dream will give you a sense of purpose and direction. God gives us dreams to give us a sense of purpose.

It is sad that many people, including Christians, do not have a sense of purpose or direction. They are satisfied with mediocrity or - at best - an average life. God has much more for us. We have been put on earth for a purpose. God has an agenda for your life. You are here on a mission. Your dream will bring meaning and purpose into your life.

The book of Genesis in the Bible tells the story of Joseph and his dreams of greatness. Joseph was the eleventh of the twelve sons of Jacob. When he was a teenager he had two dreams. In the first dream he saw himself and his brothers gathering bundles of grain. Suddenly, his bundle stood upright and all the bundles of grain gathered around his bundle and bowed down to it. In the second dream he saw the sun, the moon, and eleven stars bowing down to him. These are incredible dreams. When he told his brothers and his father, his brothers hated him; his father thought they were bizarre dreams. However, they were dreams of Joseph's future. God used the dreams to reveal His plans and purpose to Joseph. He was destined for greatness and significance. Although he would go through trials and tribulation, he persevered. God strengthened him in faith despite his humiliating experiences before the fulfilment of the dreams.

Your dream will give you the courage to overcome obstacles or adversities and make you achieve the impossible. Abraham and Sarah were old. Sarah had passed the age of childbearing. However, God gave Abraham a big dream, a dream that seemed impossible in the eyes of men. In Genesis 15, God showed Abraham the stars of the heaven and challenged him to count the stars, and said that that's how big and numerous his family would be. Abraham believed God, he believed that he would be a father, a natural father and spiritual father to numerous people all over the earth.

Friend, never allow your age, gender, nationality, background, education or even inexperience to limit the size of your dream.

I read about a young boy, James Mastronado who had a big dream for his home state – Ohio, US. In the 1950s, the state organised a contest to select a new motto. James, who was twelve years old at that time, suggested that "With God all things are possible" be adopted as the state motto. He campaigned for about three years for his dream. His dream became a reality in July 1959 when the state of Ohio adopted "With God all things are possible" as the state motto.

Surely, with God all things are possible. God is able to fulfil your dreams. He is able to make your dream a reality. That is why you should not limit yourself. You are capable of great accomplishments. Your relatives or close associates may despise you and undermine your dream, I encourage you to keep your dream alive. God delights in your dream and He wants to help you. God would not have put a dream or desire in your heart that He is unable to accomplish.

In 1 Samuel 3, the Bible described how a young boy Samuel, received a vision from God. This was a time of spiritual dryness in Israel. The vision God gave Samuel was bold and breath-taking. God revealed to him that He was going to judge the then priest, Eli, and his children because of the sins of Eli's children. Samuel was young and inexperienced at the time when God revealed the vision to him. In fact he could not discern that it was the Lord calling him the first few times he heard His voice. It was Eli who discerned that it was the Lord calling him and advised him on how to respond to God's call. Although the vision judged Eli and his children, it pointed to a new life for God's people. God also used the vision to motivate young Samuel in the direction of his calling and purpose. He was to be a prophet of God. God eventually established him to provide spiritual guidance and oversight over the nation of Israel.

Right from the time that Joshua and Caleb spied on the Promised Land, they both had dreams about the land. The other ten spies saw giants, obstacles and limitations. Joshua and Caleb, on the other hand, had dreams of possessing the Promised Land. They saw themselves and their children living in the Promised Land. Their dreams were bigger than the giants. They saw beyond the threats and obstacles the giants might pose. God honoured their faith and dreams by promising to preserve their lives to possess the Promised Land. The other ten spies, the naysayers, negative and faithless would not be able to enter the promise land. They would die in the wilderness.

God kept His promise to Joshua and Caleb and preserved their lives. Forty-five years after they had spied on the Promised Land, Caleb came to Joshua, who had been appointed a leader after the death of Moses. He reminded Joshua of the promise that God made to both of them regarding their inheritance. He told Joshua that even at 85 years of age, he was as strong and fit for war as he was at 40. He boldly requested the land of Hebron, the inheritance promised by God. He was willing to drive out the giants, the Anakims - the inhabitants of Hebron. In Joshua 14:6-15, the Bible recorded the assertive way in which he told Joshua *"I am as strong this day as I was in the day that Moses sent me. As my strength was then, even so is my strength now, for war, both to go out, and to come in."* How incredible, at 85! I have heard many people say that life begins at 40. For Caleb, life actually began at 85. Your dream will give you energy and strength. Your dream will give you your youth back.

A few years ago, my wife and I were in Dublin for the 70th birthday of my dear friend, Paddy Keegan. It was a surprise party organised by his wife, Pauline. Paddy and Pauline are Pastors in a striving multicultural Church in Dublin. They are also leaders in the network marketing business and have been the number one retailer of Forever Living products in the whole of Ireland for many years. At the party, after Paddy had gotten over the initial surprise of realising Pauline had lured him to the hotel to execute her hidden agenda; I heard Paddy saying to a couple "I don't feel like I am 70. I feel much younger. I feel like I am just starting. I will continue to live until I die". That's how dreamers talk. They are full of faith and energy. They are positive. They think, talk and act on possibilities. They look beyond their limitations. They are focused, active and make good use of their time. They think about the next project, the next target, the next customer, the next sale, and the next level. While they are thankful about their present accomplishments, they are yearning for the next level, higher level. That is the power of dreams, so dream big!

Why Dream Big?

The late Napoleon Hill, an American author and one of the earliest producers of personal success literature, said "You can be anything you want to be if you believe with sufficient conviction and act in accordance with your faith; for whatever the mind can conceive and believe - it can achieve".

Pablo Picasso, a Spanish painter and sculptor in the 20th Century, also said "Everything you can imagine is real". Yes, whatever you can imagine in your mind is real and achievable. Everything you see around you is a product of someone's dreams and imaginations. You too can imagine and achieve great things. You can accomplish big dreams. Why not think big? Why think little when you can achieve much? When you dream big, you open your life to numerous possibilities.

In Ephesians 3, the Bible states that God is able to do immeasurably more than we ask or imagine, according to His power that is at work within us. When you dream big, you set yourself up for extraordinary help from God. You end up achieving much more than you ever thought you could.

The good thing about dreaming big is that it pushes you out of your comfort zone. It draws out of you strengths, gifts and potentials that may have been lying dormant in you. It enlarges your mind. It takes you from the land of mediocre to an adventure of possibility and personal development.

Most of the great improvements and solutions to human problems are possible because of people who dared to dream big. Think of men like Alexander Graham Bell, a Scottish scientist who invented the first practical telephone; Thomas Edison, who created an electric light bulb; the Wright brothers, who invented and built the world's first successful airplane; and Alexander Fleming, a biologist and pharmacologist who first invented penicillin, making the start of modern antibiotics.

You've probably heard of Rosa Parks, an African American civil rights activist whom the US congress called "The First Lady of Civil Rights." In December 1955, Rosa Park refused to give up her bus seat to a white passenger. She was arrested for violating the then laws of segregation known as the 'Jim Crow law'. However, her act of defiance began a movement that ended legal segregation in America and made her an inspiration to freedom loving people all over the world.

Another woman, Mother Teresa, made a mark internationally in charitable works. She founded the Missionaries of Charity, a Roman Catholic religious congregation dedicated to helping the poor and needy. It began as a small community with twelve members in Calcutta, India. Today it has over 4,500 Sisters running orphanages, hospices, and charity centres worldwide.

The dreams of these men and women of faith have made the world a better place to live. How do you want to improve the world? What legacy do you want to leave on earth in your remembrance? What legacy do you want to leave behind that will make a real difference?

Your dream may be the key to positive change to your family, community and the world at large. Your dream will connect you to your inner self and draw out of your soul a greater purpose.

Making Your Dream Come True

There is nothing more fulfilling and rewarding as a dream that comes true. You can imagine how Leona Lewis felt when her dream of becoming a music superstar became a reality when she won The X Factor in 2006. Tears of excitement flowed freely from her eyes. Imagine within 30 minutes of the announcement, there were 50,000 downloads of her album, half a million sales in the first week and 20 million sales worldwide. What a reward! You also have the 'X factor' and much more. You have 'God's factor', for with God all things are possible. You are capable of achieving your dreams and aspirations if you believe!

One of the reasons why some people do not realise their dreams and aspirations is that they do not really believe in their dreams. Deep down, they do not believe they are good enough, talented, bright or experienced enough to do great things. They allow their self-limiting beliefs to rob them of the prospect of their dreams. Some allow critics and naysayers to persuade them they are not good enough and capable of achieving their dreams. They give in to voices that say:

"Don't fool yourself"
"You can't possibly do that"
"Many people have tried and failed"
"Why take a risk?"
"I also wanted to do that, but realised it's not possible"
"How are you going to get the finances?"
"Who do you think you are?"

If you want to see you dream come true, you have to believe you are capable of accomplishing it. Don't give in to self-limiting thoughts and negative voices of men.

In Chapter 2 of this book, I wrote about David's understanding of the value placed on him by God. He did not give in to the intimidation and undermining words of his brother Eliab when he wanted to fight Goliath. David had a dream: to slay Goliath, the enemy of God's people. He believed in his God-given ability and, more importantly, he trusted God to help him. He would not allow anyone to intimidate him. He walked away from his brother Eliab when he spoke negatively to him, trying to discourage him from taking up the challenge of Goliath. You may read the story in 1 Samuel 17.

Like David, you may also need to turn away from people who do not believe in your dream, including relatives, friends and associates. It's not their dream, it's yours. You better believe in your dream. No one can truly believe for you. You see, you dream may be so big that it may even scare you. You may not know how it could happen. With men it may be impossible, but with God all things are possible.

Visualise Your Dream

About six months before I started writing, I had a picture of the finished book in my mind. I imagined the glossy cover with beautiful design of a crown. I saw the book in the hands of many people, young and old all over the nations. Even in places I may not physically reach. I felt the excitement that people would experience for the insight, inspiration, encouragements and comfort they will receive through this writing. I could imagine the sense of appreciation in the hearts of many people for access to this book and benefits of a life changing experience. I felt so strongly about the images and pictures being formed in my mind as if it were real.

Visualisation is one of the quickest ways to manifest your dream. It is having a vivid and compelling image or picture in your mind about the objects of your desire, dream or aspiration. You can vividly imagine in your mind and see yourself functioning in your dream career, living in your dream house or carrying your baby. Visualising imprints your dream or aspiration in your mind. It's the paintbrush that designs beautiful and attractive pictures and images of your dream in your mind. When you visualise, you immerse your thoughts and imaginary senses into your dream.

Focus your thoughts on positive images and positive outcomes rather that negatives. Your thoughts have vibrations, both positive and negative. Positive images will attract positive vibrations, which will usually attract good and helpful things and people to you. On the other hand negative images will attract negative things. Visualise on possibilities, goodwill and benefits rather that impossibilities and problems.

Visualisation will also help increase your motivation and determination to take positive steps and actions. By visualising, you can also get creative ideas that will help you achieve your dream. Visualisation empowers your mind. As pictures or images and the benefits of your dream are formed in your mind, you will become more active and alert to information, resources and opportunities that will help you achieve your dream. Visualisation can be a vital key to fulfilling your dream.

Create a Plan of Action

Once you visualise your dream, you should create a plan to accomplish it. Your plan is the road map that you will follow to realise your dream. Planning will help you decide what things to do, identify people that might help you, determine resources, skills and knowledge and information that you may need. Planning will also help you identify potential obstacles and possible solutions and ways that you might overcome the obstacles. Commit your plan into writing. This will serve as a point of reference for you as you go along.

Take Action

Visualising your dream and creating the best action plan will not do much in achieving your dream unless you take action to make them happen. You have to put your foot to the pedal, start the ignition and move steadily towards fulfilment of your dream.

Visualisation, goal setting and having a plan of action will motivate you and help you clarify actions you need to take to fulfil your dreams, but you need to take those actions. Actions are what turn imagination into reality. It is when you start taking actions that miracles start happening. Following our dreams with action is usually the hardest part of the journey. This is where most people give up, abandon their dreams due to fear, insecurities, obstacles, temporary failures and setbacks. They throw in the towel early! Taking actions requires commitment, discipline and persistence.

Shun those legitimate excuses that people make to postpone actions or even totally abandon their dreams. Excuses such as:

"I don't have enough time"
"I am too busy"
"I am still young"
"I am too old"
"I have no experience"
"I am not ready"
"There is no one to help"
"No one wants to support me"
"There is not enough money"

In Ecclesiastes 11:4, the Bible records a profound statement made by King Solomon, who was renowned for his wisdom and insight. The Amplified Bible puts it this way: *"He who observes the wind (and waits for all conditions to be favourable) will not sow, and he regards the clouds will not reap."*

The New Living Translation Bible puts it this way: *"Farmers who wait for perfect weather never plant. If they watch every cloud, they never harvest."*

Some people expect circumstances to be perfect and want to anticipate all results. These people are like farmers who always look to wind and weather and miss the time of sowing and reaping. Of course it does not mean that you should ignore your situation.

You do not need to wait until your situation is perfect before taking actions on your dream. The truth is the situation will never be perfect. If you wait for perfect conditions you will never take any action on your dream. Start doing something now towards fulfilling your dream. Don't procrastinate. Following your dream with actions can be tough, but you will find it exciting and rewarding if you don't give up.

CHAPTER SEVEN

TAKE A STEP OF FAITH

Taking a step out in faith is not the easiest thing to do, but it is the surest route to fulfilling your dreams and destiny.

God called a man named Abraham to leave his homeland and go to a place that He would show him. God promised that He would bless him and make him and his family great. Abraham stepped out in faith based on God's promise. God did not tell him immediately where the place was, but He assured him He would make the place known to him. In obedience to God, Abraham took a bold step, took his wife along with his nephew on a journey to the place where he would become great and significant. He left behind his friends, acquaintances, extended family, native town, country and embarked on a journey to a place he had never been before. God led Abraham to the land of Canaan, blessed him and he became prosperous. He had many cattle, servants and a great household. The Bible confirms in Genesis 24 that the Lord blessed Abraham in every way. One of his closest servants, Eliezer, attested to the goodness of God in the life of Abraham. He stated *'The LORD has blessed my master abundantly, and he has become wealthy. He has given him sheep and cattle, silver and gold, male and female servants, and camels and donkeys.'*

Many people are afraid to step out in faith when they get prompted by God. They are afraid to take action because they cannot see what is on the other side. However, faith does not mean we have to see the clear path or the whole picture before we take bold actions. Dr Martin Luther King puts it this way, "Faith is taking the first step even when you can't see the whole staircase". Faith is confidence in God who is all-knowing, all-powerful, wise, and an all-sufficient God.

After feeding the 5,000, Jesus sent His disciples ahead of Him in a boat to cross the Sea of Galilee. When everyone had left, Jesus went up to the mountainside by Himself to pray. By the time He finished praying, it was early in the morning. He came to the seashore looking for His disciples and saw them in a boat far away. He decided to walk on the water towards their boat. This terrified the disciples. They thought they were seeing a ghost. Knowing they were frightened, He called on them saying *"Take courage! It is I. Don't be afraid."* Peter, one of His disciples, replied *"Lord, if it's really you, tell me to come to you on the water"* (Matthew 14:28). Jesus responded *"Come"*, with His hands stretched out towards Peter.

The other disciples watched as Peter got out of the boat and began to walk on the water towards Jesus. Jesus invited Peter to come. Peter got out of the boat and began walking on the water toward Jesus. Oh, that was a bold step of faith! Peter took an action by stepping out of the boat. I can imagine what was going on in Peter's mind when Jesus said to them *"Take courage! It is I. Don't be afraid."* Peter, probably thought *"This is great stuff that Jesus is doing, I hope I sure can! If it's the Lord, I am sure He will make it possible for me too."* Peter knew that with God, all things are possible. He was convinced that with the Word from the Lord, he could step out of the boat by faith.

Friend, in order to step out in faith, you have to conceive a vision of possibilities in your heart. You may not have to walk on water like Peter did, but God may be calling you to new possibilities. It may be that you need to start a new career, a new business, a new course, learn a new skill, start a new project, write a book, record a song, move to a new place, build or buy a new house, or begin a new relationship. Whatever it is, possibilities are within reach. You just need to see them.

When Jesus told Peter to "Come", Peter had to come out of the boat in order to walk towards Jesus. He had to leave the other disciples in the boat. Your step of faith will move you out of your comfort zone. Your step of faith may even require that you change some friends and associates. You need to move away from negative people and connect with positive, faith-filled people. When Peter moved out of the boat where the other disciples were and started moving towards Jesus, a storm arose and he began to sink. He had to cry to Jesus for help. Immediately Jesus stretched His hands towards him. Many times when we go through problems, the storms of life and challenges, the people close to us can make all the difference. They can help us through and out of the problems, while other people can compound the problems.

Taking a step of faith may mean you have to try again despite any previous disappointments, setbacks, rejections or failures.

In Luke 5, the Bible gives an account of another positive step of faith taken by Peter. Jesus entered a boat owned by Simon Peter and started preaching to a multitude on the shore of the Sea of Galilee. After His sermon, Jesus said to Peter *"Launch out into the deep and let down your nets for a catch"*.

Peter was a professional fisherman. He and his colleagues had exhausted all their expertise and fishing techniques without positive results. They toiled all night but caught nothing. Not even a single fish! It seemed they have wasted all their time, efforts and resources. It was a hopeless situation. Peter now had a choice to make; take a step of faith by obeying Jesus' command, or give up all hope. His common sense was probably telling him, "Peter, do you want to put yourself through more stress and pain? You've already toiled all night, wasted all your energy and resources, with nothing to show for it. Try again? Are you a fool? It cannot work out. Forget it. In fact, better abandon it all!" On the other hand, something deep within his heart must have been telling him, "This is my time for a turnaround, this is my time for success, this is my time for restoration. I just need to trust and obey His Word. I've heard Him preach the Word of hope and faith. I won't give up, I will trust and obey. At His word I will take a step of faith. I will try again, this time will be different. This is my time for breakthrough. I'll go for it!"

Peter took that step of faith and the results were extraordinary. The Bible states that when Peter and his colleagues launched out into the deep and caught so much fish that their nets were breaking. They had to call other ships over to help them carry the overflow of fish.

You may be wondering: is it worth trying again, after all, it did not work out the first, second or maybe even third time? Don't be afraid. God is saying to you now: take that step of faith. Launch out again. Peter had a previous experience of toiling all night without catching nothing; nevertheless, at the word of God, he took a step of faith and he experienced extraordinary success. I don't know what previous experience or setback you have had. Maybe it was a failed relationship, failed business, bankruptcy or liquidated assets. It could be you have just recently lost your job, experienced setbacks in your studies or project. It may even be a serious health issue. Fear not. Take a step of faith.

In Luke Chapter 8, the Bible gives an account of a certain woman suffering from the flow of blood for twelve years. She had suffered a great deal under the care of many doctors and had spent all she had, yet instead of getting better she grew worse. Finally, she heard about Jesus and made up her mind she would reach out to him by faith believing she would be healed. As Jesus was passing by, a crowd of people followed him. However, the woman was determined. She came behind Jesus in the crowd and touched His garment. Immediately, her bleeding stopped. Although Jesus could not have seen her when she touched his cloth – due to the crowd around – Jesus knew immediately that power had gone out of Him. He turned to the crowd around and said, *"Who touched my clothes?"* The woman, knowing what had happened to her, came trembling and fell down before Him and told why she had touched Him and how she was instantly healed. Jesus commended her for her faith. He said to her, *"Daughter, your faith has healed you. Go in peace."*

She was a woman of faith and action. Despite disappointment from previous medical treatments, financial strains, shame and possibly rejections and loneliness, the woman was determined because she had heard about Jesus. She must have heard how Jesus gave sight to the blind, opened the ears of the deaf, made the lame to walk, raised the dead, delivered the demon possessed and multiplied food to the multitudes. She decided to take a step of faith and expected a change in her situation.

Mark records the thoughts of this woman before she touched the clothes of Jesus in chapter 5 verse 28. The woman said to herself *"If I can touch His clothes, I will be healed."* She saw possibilities; she expected to be healed and took that bold step of faith. And she was healed!

Whatever issue you have been battling for years – it may be depression, financial issues, childlessness, marital problems, loneliness, low self-confidence or addiction – I am sure like the woman with issue of blood, you must have heard about God's faithfulness from the testimonies of others. It's time to take faith-based action. Fear not, take a bold step of faith. When you take a step of faith following God's prompting, despite your past experience, limitations or setbacks, you will step into a whole new experience. You will accomplish things you have never accomplished before. You will experience a turnaround in your situation. God will turn your place of defeat into a place of victory for you. He will turn your failures to success, and lack to abundance and fruitfulness. Oh, you will experience progress like never before! Each step you take will be a miracle step.

So many Christians are simply folding their arms, praying and hoping their situation changes. But God is actually waiting for them to take positive actions, trusting Him to release the grace, resources, favour and guidance they need along the way.

How I got my First Job as a Solicitor

After graduating from University, I set out to pursue my dream of travelling to America instead of looking for a job at a law firm. However, things did not work out according to my plans as I was refused a visa to travel to America. I was very disappointment as I had no other plans at that time. After a few months of self-pity and feeling discouraged, I decided to seek employment in a law firm. For about a week I had a strong and constant urge to visit a friend named Gbola, who I knew back from university. He had graduated two years before me. He was working as a solicitor in the most reputable law firm in another city, about an hour from where I lived. I finally decided to visit Gbola. Within two days, I made arrangements to visit him in his office.

When I met Gbola, I told him I was looking for work in a law firm. He informed me of a vacancy in another reputable law firm in the city. He had met one of the senior lawyers in court the previous day who informed him they had an immediate vacancy for a solicitor. Gbola suggested I should visit the law firm immediately and apply in person. As soon I left his office, I decided to go straight to the law firm to try my luck. Within twenty minutes I was waiting to be interviewed by the senior partner in the law firm. The interview lasted fifteen minutes. The law firm was seeking a young solicitor who would be available to start work immediately. To my surprise I was offered the vacancy and within one week I started working as a solicitor in that law firm. I believe it was God that ordered my steps. If I had ignored the urge I had to visit my friend, I would probably have missed the opportunity that was awaiting me.

Take Risks

Sometimes your steps of faith may involve making decisions, choices or taking actions that involve risk.

By nature, a risk is uncertain, unpredictable and sometimes frightening. You may fail, experience loss, face criticism, rejection, demotion, persecution, or even put your life on the line for your decisions or actions.

Most people prefer to maintain the status quo stay in their comfort zones and totally avoid taking risks. Without taking risks, you may never experience the potential of what it could be, or you may get stuck in what it's always been. As Leo Buscaglia puts it, "The person who risks nothing, does nothing, has nothing, is nothing and becomes nothing. He may avoid suffering and sorrow, but he simply cannot learn and feel and change and grow and love and live".

The Bible tells the story of a young, beautiful, Jewish woman named Esther who risked her life to save her people from destruction in Persia. Esther was chosen to be a Queen in replacement of Vashti, who rebelled against the King's command to appear before his royal majesty.

Esther had a cousin by the name Mordecai, a minor official in the Persian government. Mordecai was a loyal and faithful official. His once uncovered a plot to assassinate the King and told Esther about it. The plot was thwarted and the King's life was spared.

On another occasion, Haman, one of the King's highest official, devised a scheme to have every Jew in Persia killed. Somehow, he succeeded in getting the King to issue a decree to annihilate all the Jews on a specific day. When Mordecai learned about Haman's wicked plot, he quickly sent message to Esther about the plan and implored her to intervene on behalf of her people, the Jews. When Esther got the message she was very concerned for the Jews. However, she had a challenge. According to the palace protocol, no one can approach the King without being summoned by the King himself. Whoever attempts to approach the King uninvited would be killed. Although Esther was the Queen, the King had not summoned her in the last thirty days. Initially Esther was reluctant to approach the King. However, following Mordecai's insistence, she resolved to risk her life and took the much needed step of faith to approach the King. The Bible records Esther's resolution in Esther 4:15-17: *'I will go to the king, even though it is against the law. And if I perish, I perish."*

Although Esther did not know what the outcome would be, she took the risk of approaching the King. Indeed she found favour with the King. The Bible records what happened in Chapter 5:

"On the third day, Esther put on her royal robes and stood in the inner court of the palace, in front of the king's hall. The king was sitting on his royal throne in the hall, facing the entrance. When he saw Queen Esther standing in the court, he was pleased with her and held out to her the gold sceptre that was in his hand. So Esther approached and touched the tip of the sceptre. Then the king asked, "What is it, Queen Esther? What is your request? Even up to half the kingdom, it will be given you."

Esther eventually pleaded with the King to avert the evil plan of Haman to destroy her people. The King granted her request and immediately overruled the original verdict to execute the Jews. Instead Haman was executed. The Jews were saved from execution because of Esther's intervention.

Esther took a risk and delivered her people from destruction. Friend, God may also be calling you to take a risk that will turn around your life, family or loved ones. Are you willing to count the cost and take the risk anyway?

The Power of Forgiveness

Many people try to take a step of faith but have not learnt to walk in forgiveness. Taking steps of faith may require that you forgive or reconcile with a valued friend, spouse, partner, father, mother, son, daughter, brother, sister, colleague, business associate or anyone who has offended you.

Forgiveness is not always easy, especially when we have been betrayed, lied about, abandoned, abused or taken advantage of by people we trusted. As humans we tend not to forgive easily. We're quick to justify our action based on the wrong we have suffered. After all, it was not our fault. We didn't deserve the unjust treatment, the abandonment, rejection, abuse or ill treatments! The truth is you may never experience true peace and happiness by holding on to offences.

Sometime ago, someone close to me spoke to me in a manner that I found offensive. I was angry, broken, discouraged and felt undermined. For the next two days, I focused on my hurts. I struggled with the thought of letting go of the offence, though I knew I had to forgive. I finally let go of the offence and resentment in my heart. Immediately my spirit was revived, peace and joy flooded my heart. Of course that was not the only time when I have been hurt by people. There were times when I thought I have gotten over a certain hurt, then something else happened: another hurt, another misunderstanding, ill treatment or disloyalty that I had to deal with. I thank God for the grace to overcome and I am still looking to Him for grace to always love and forgive people that may offend me.

Unfortunately, many people have made bitterness and hatred their advocates. They employ bitterness and hatred as prosecutors to press for the highest possible punishment for those that offend or wrong them in any way. Kris Vallatton in his book, *"The Supernatural Power of Forgiveness"* states "Regardless of why you've made bitterness and hatred your best friends, if you carry them along long enough, they will eventually eat you from the inside out."

Holding on to offences and bitterness is dangerous. They lock people in regret and resentment over the past. When I was in secondary school, as a literature student I enjoyed reading Charles Dickens novels. One of his novels titled *"Great Expectations"* has a very interesting and bizarre character - Miss Havisham.

Miss Havisham is a wealthy spinster who lives in her ruined mansion with her adopted daughter, Estella. Miss Havisham's mother died when she was a baby. Growing up, she was spoilt by her father, a wealthy brewer. As an adult, she inherited her father's fortune and fell in love with a man named Compeyson, who was only out to swindle her of her riches. Her cousin, Matthew Pocket, warned her to be careful, but she was too much in love to listen. On the wedding day, while she was dressing, Miss Havisham received a letter from Compeyson and realised he had defrauded her and she had been left at the altar.

Humiliated and heartbroken, from that day on, she remained alone in her decaying mansion, Satis House, never removing her wedding dress, wearing only one shoe, leaving the wedding breakfast and cake uneaten on the table and allowing only a few people to see her. She even had all of the clocks in her mansion stopped at twenty minutes to nine – the exact time when she had received the disappointing letter from Compeyson. She remains in her world of pain, regret and bitterness for many years. She adopts Estella, the daughter of a convict, for the purpose of breaking the hearts of men as a vicarious revenge for her pain.

Friend, whatever hurt, disappointment or abuse you have experienced, do not be like Miss Havisham. Don't allow bitterness and disappointments to hold you in the past. God has a better future in store for you. Let go of the past, let go of the disappointments.

Some are of the opinion that forgiveness depicts weakness. This is far from true. Being able to forgive is definitely a sign of strength and grace. Robert Enright, an educational psychology professor renowned for his exploration into the role of forgiveness, believes that learning to forgive is not a weakness at all – but a powerful act that brings healing and happiness. "[Forgiveness] does not make you weak," Enright affirmed "The love you cultivate and develop in your heart is stronger than any injustices anyone can ever throw against you. And once you live that, you realise how very, very strong you can be, because that's a buffer against all of the poison that unfortunately visits us just by being alive".

Forgiveness is powerful. It can heal deep wounds and hurts. I recently read a true life story of a hospice nurse, Wanda, who was reunited with her long-lost father whom she had not met in 41 years. Her father, Victor, left the family when Wanda was just a baby. Her mother raised her and her sister on her own in New York. For many years Wanda wondered about her father, what he looked like and where he could be. All she knew was his name.

When Wanda grew up, she became a hospice nurse at the Calvary Hospital in the Bronx, where she would help provide medicine and comfort to patients in their final days. One evening, Wanda was on her regular shift when a terminally ill cancer patient was brought to her ward. She overheard one of the doctors mentioning the patient's name over the phone; she became curious, wondering if that could be her father. She searched his medical chart for more information about his age and also went to the patient's room to chat with him to be sure if he was actually her long-lost father. When Wanda asked him if he had any children, his response immediately let her know that he was indeed her father. It was a miraculous moment for both of them. They could not imagine how gracious God could be, joining their two paths together again. Wanda's father regretted the past and asked her to forgive him for not been a good dad. Wanda responded to her father by saying "I forgive you; the past is in the past. You can't change the past. I love you".

Some people would have used this opportunity to settle old scores with their father. This was not Wanda's attitude. She had no interest in dwelling on the past. She was more interested in catching up with her father and creating new memories with him. Wanda's reaction to her father was touching. She forgave and showed him love and care. Although her father only had a short time to live, her forgiveness and their father-daughter reunion brought him peace. Wanda' ability to forgive and love is so inspiring. She is a shining example of forgiveness and grace. I admire her courage and love. I hope you will learn some lessons from her beautiful heart. I surely did.

Forgive Yourself

Forgiveness is beautiful when you give it as a gift to others, whether they deserve it or not. However, you have to learn to give yourself this beautiful gift of love and mercy as well. Unfortunately, some people have a hard time forgiving themselves. They inflict themselves with unwarranted pain and feel they deserve to suffer for what they did wrong.

Debbie was very lucky to get a job a marketing executive in a shipping company soon after graduating from university. She was promoted to marketing supervisor after three years. She quit her job after working in her new role for two years to purse a master's degree. Her parents had advised her not to resign her job. They advised her to enrol for a part-time master's or consider a distance learning program. Her best friend and two of her work colleagues also tried to persuade her not to resign. However, she had made up her mind and would not even consider their advice.

Unfortunately, things did not work out according to Debbie's plans. Her master's program was prolonged due to financial strains and an unexpected pregnancy. She had to defer her studies for three years to take care of her baby. She managed to continue her studies after three years and finally earned her master's degree. She applied to return to her former company after her masters, but her application was rejected. She also applied to other companies and attended several job interviews without success. After about three years of being jobless, she regretted her decision to resign her first job. She became depressed, withdrawn and miserable. She continually blamed herself for quitting her job concluding that she ruined her own life. She even attempted suicide by taking a drug overdose on one occasion. She felt she was a failure that did not deserve to live. She could not imagine why she did not consider the advice given by her parents and colleagues before resigning her first job. She continually told her mother "I cannot forgive myself for quitting my first job".

Sometimes the most difficult person to forgive is ourselves, especially when we make mistakes or do something wrong. However, learning to forgive yourself is a sure step of faith that will bring you peace and contentment.

J. Johnson observed that "In every single person's life lies a mistake made by a person that they wish they could take back, whether they admit it or not. The only way to move past the regret of the mistake in our lives that still causes us pain is to forgive yourself for it. Not only is it our right to, but forgiving ourselves allows us to move past obstacles in our lives that we would not have otherwise moved past without doing so".

Perhaps you have made mistakes, foolish decisions, or committed a sin that you thought you cannot forgive yourself for. It's time to set yourself free. It's time to let go of whatever you are holding against yourself and move on with your life. When you make mistakes or commit a sin, it is important you acknowledge your sin or mistake, feel remorse, repent and learn from your mistake or error so that you do not keep repeating the same mistake or sin. However, you do not have to keep beating yourself up about the past.

The Bible states in 1st John 1:9 that *"If we confess our sins, God is faithful and just to forgive us our sins and purge us of all unrighteousness"*. God is loving and merciful. When you sincerely confess your sins or admit a fault, God moves on. He no longer holds your sins or mistake against you. However, until you learn to forgive yourself, it can feel like God has not yet forgiven you. You need to free yourself from the burden of guilt and hardness you have placed on yourself and receive the flow of the unconditional love of God.

Forgiving ourselves is not about justifying our sins or wrongdoings. Sometimes we may have to experience the pain of our wrongdoings or make restitutions if necessary, but self-forgiveness will open our lives to healing and restorations.

David, the second King of Israel, was one of the most remarkable men that ever lived. He was best known as 'a man after God's heart'. After removing Saul as King, God testified concerning him *"I have found David son of Jesse, a man after My own heart, who will do all My will."* From childhood, David had absolute faith in God. As a young shepherd boy, he fearlessly challenged and killed Goliath, the captain of the Philistines in the battlefield, thereby becoming the most respected military captain in Israel. Despite being anointed by God to be King, he endured years of persecution from King Saul and patiently waited for God to give him the promised throne. When he became King, he united the twelve tribes of Israel into a great Kingdom. He defeated the enemies of Israel especially the Philistines and Moabites. The Bible records in 2 Samuel 8:15 *"So David reigned over Israel; and David administers judgement and justice to all his people."*

In spite of his great achievements and love for God. David was not without fault or sinless. In 2 Samuel Chapter 11, the Bible records that King David sent his army to wage war, but he himself stayed behind in Jerusalem. One evening, King David was relaxing on his palace balcony when he saw a beautiful woman bathing in her house. Through his messengers, he learned the woman's name was Bathsheba, wife of Uriah, a member of Israel's army who had gone to battle. Inflamed with passion, King David sent for Bathsheba and committed adultery with her.

Not long after their illicit affair, Bathsheba sent message to King David, telling him that she was pregnant. When the King learnt about the pregnancy, he determined to conceal his sin. He immediately recalled Uriah from the battlefront and told him to take some leave, hoping that Uriah would visit his wife at home. He planned to attribute Bathsheba's pregnancy to her husband so that when the child was born it would appear as if it was Uriah's. However, he didn't go home. Instead he stayed within the palace barracks. Although King David tried to persuade him to visit his wife at home, Uriah, being a patriotic soldier, told the King he would not indulge in matrimonial pleasure when his fellow soldiers are in the battlefield. King David then invited Uriah for dinner and got him drunk, hoping that intoxication will arouse Uriah's desire for his wife. However, his plan was unsuccessful; Uriah did not go home to his wife.

Finally, King David became desperate. He wanted to hide his sin at all cost. He sent Uriah back to the battlefield with a letter he has written Joab, the captain of Israel's army. In the letter the king instructed Joab, to put Uriah in the front lines where the fighting is fiercest. The troops were to withdraw, leaving Uriah undefended so that he might be slain. Unfortunately Uriah had no idea of the underserved death sentence on him. Joab carried out the King's instructions and Uriah was killed in the battle. But King David's action displeased the Lord.

God sent Nathan the prophet to reprove King David of his sin. When Nathan got to the King, he related to him the parable of a rich man who took away the one little ewe lamb of his poor neighbour. Hearing the parable, King David's anger was excited in judgement against the unrighteous deed of the rich man. That was the moment the prophet decided to call a spade a spade. Nathan applied the case directly to David's actions with regards to Bathsheba and her husband Uriah, making it clear to him that God was sorely displeased with his actions. King David immediately confessed his sin, expressed sincere repentance and admitted responsibility for his wicked actions. King David had to endure the severe punishments of his actions. The child born by Bathsheba after the illicit affair was struck with severe illness and died few days after his birth. About a year later, Absalom, one of David's sons led an insurrection that led to civil war in the Kingdom.

Truly the sin committed by David was grievous, however, God forgave him. You need to read Psalm 51 to understand the depth of David's remorsefulness about his sin. He prayed to God to wash him thoroughly of his iniquity and cleanse him from his sin. He pleaded to God to create a new heart within him, a heart filled with clean thoughts and right desires. He also asked God to restore joy of salvation to him. Obviously, his sin had created heaviness, guilty and self-condemnation in him. God forgave him and in answer to his prayers, God lifted the weight and burden of guilt from his heart and restored peace and joy to his heart.

Friend, you cannot change your past mistakes and errors. However, you can be free from the pain of the past and face your future with hope and faith if you repent of your sins and errors. As God forgave David and restored peace into his heart, God will do the same to you if you sincerely repent, seek God for forgiveness and restoration. Accept God's forgiveness by forgiving yourself. Self-forgiveness releases the grace of God that makes us an overcomer rather than the victim of our own errors. When you forgive yourself and others, you free yourself to take steps of faith.

CHAPTER EIGHT

THE FRINGE BENEFITS OF FAILURE

I saw an interesting diagram of a man who was about to climb the stairway to success. The stairway has seven steps. The first three steps has an inscription of failure. At the top is success. He had to climb through failure in order to reach the top.

No one likes to fail. Failure can be agonising, stressful and emotionally hard to bear. But failure is part of life. In your life journeys, you will experience failure. You always pass failure on the way to success. However, failing is not the same as being a failure. Failure is an experience. If you haven't failed, you have little experience.

JK Rowling, the author of the best-selling Harry Potter novels, saw herself as the biggest failure seven years after graduating from university. Her marriage had failed, she was jobless, severely depressed, and with a dependent child. In her commencement address at the Annual Meeting of Harvard Alumni Association in June 2008, she described her failure as liberating. In her own words, "Failure meant a stripping away of the inessential. I stopped pretending to myself that I was anything other than what I was, and began to direct all my energy into finishing the only work that mattered to me. Had I really succeeded in anything else, I might never have found the determination to succeed in the one arena I believed I truly belonged. I was set free, because my greatest fear had been realised, and I was still alive, and still had a daughter whom I adored, and I had an old type writer and a big idea. Failure gave me the inner security that I had never attained by passing examinations. Failure taught me things about myself that I could have learned no other way. I discovered that I had a strong will, and more discipline than I had suspected, I also found out that I had friends whose value was truly above the price of rubies".

Despite a disadvantaged background and failures, JK Rowling progressed from living on social security to multi-millionaire status within five years. Her Harry Potter books have gained worldwide attention, won multiple awards, sold over 400 million copies to become the best-selling book series in history, as well as being the basis for a popular series of films in which Rowling had overall approval on the scripts. Forbes has named Rowling the first person to become a U.S. dollar billionaire from writing books.

Successful people learn by failing. Sometimes by failing again and again until they eventually get it right. Many people give up after a few attempts but those who don't give up are the ones who learn new things.

Peter J Daniels is an unusual man of faith and determination. Born in Australia, his parents were third generation welfare recipients. He was used to being poor. He attended elementary school in Adelaide, Australia, however, because of a learning disability, he struggled to read and write. Consequently he was labelled stupid by teachers who didn't care enough to find out why he struggled. One teacher in particular, Miss Phillips would make him stand and scold him saying: "Peter Daniels, you are a bad boy and you'll never amount to anything".

This affected his self-esteem. He failed every grade in school and left aged 14 to become an apprentice bricklayer. At age 26, he was hopelessly in debt. But thanks be to God, he attended one of Billy Graham's crusades where he gave his life to Christ. He decided to go into business. The first venture failed miserably and he was broke within a year. He went into business a second time and was broke again within two years. He went into business again and became broke a third time. Most people would have given up at this point. Not Peter Daniel. His attitude was "I'm learning". He went into business a fourth time and built a successful real estate business in Australia and South East Asia. Today he is an internationally acclaimed businessman who has created successful ventures in many countries around the world. His family owns a private gold and silver bullion bank. He is also one of the world's most strategic planners, life coach and motivational speaker. Two companies have paid him a million dollars for advice. He is also a philanthropist who is passionate about helping others, especially Christians. He has helped turn many Christian business owners into millionaires.

Each failure adds to your experience. You gain more knowledge that will help you succeed better. You have more insight of how things should not be done. Failure will help you make a better plan if you see it as an opportunity rather than a disadvantage.

Failure is a wonderful way to learn what we do not know. You may have heard a version of the famous quote by Thomas Edison: "I have not failed, I have just found 10,000 ways that won't work. When I have eliminated the ways that will not work, I will find the way that will work." Friend, if you don't give up, despite setbacks and disappointments, you will find a way that works too. Never accept failure as final. Failure may mean delay, but it never means defeat. Henry Ford famously said "Failure is only the opportunity to begin again more intelligently". Sounds good? Failure can increase your intelligence if you are willing to learn from it.

My Personal Experience of Failure

Like many young, hopeful Africans seeking a better life, and thought America was the best place to live, I always wanted to live in America (since I was in my second year at university). Throughout my university years, I always had this fantasy of the American dream on my mind. Which other country would be better than God's own country(America)?

My American daydream almost affected my focus on my studies; however, I gained a second class degree. After my law degree and successfully completing the exams that gave me the licence to practice as a Barrister and Solicitor, I reluctantly attended the one-year compulsory youth service in Nigeria, though I did not see any sense in it. After all, I would shortly be moving to America. As soon as I completed the youth service I applied for a visa to travel to the USA. At the embassy, among other questions, the interviewing officer asked a law related question. Although I remembered being taught the principles relating to the question when I was in my second year, unfortunately I had forgotten the answer. I could not give a legal explanation to answer the question. The officer immediately told me that he would be refusing my visa application. I was very disappointed and felt like a failure, wondering why I could not explain a simple law principle at the interview, after spending five years studying for a Law degree. After an initial feeling of hopelessness, I decided to take an appointment as a junior lawyer in a law firm. Two years later I met a lady who would later become my wife. I later found out that she was British born by African parents. She was planning to move to the UK. We got married about two years later and we both decided to live in the UK.

Looking back to what seemed to be a failure to obtain a visa to move to the USA as a single young man, I can now appreciate the goodness of God. Had I travelled to US then, the chances of meeting my wife would have been very remote. I would have probably married another woman, or got hooked to the fast lifestyle in the US. It was after I took up the appointment at the law firm that I became a committed Christian and started attending regular Christian fellowships and listening to teachings that helped me lay a foundation for my Christian life.

Mark Victor Hanson and Robert G Allen in their book '*Cracking the Millionaire Code*' observed that:

"Every life pulses to the rhythm of its natural ebbs and flows, if you look back on your life and think you're not a winner, maybe it's because you haven't learned the lesson from your setback yet. Once you learn the lesson from a failure; you are a winner because you turned what appeared to be a strikeout into home run. You transform what many feel was an experience to avoid to a valuable one - turning lemons to lemonade"

Yes, I was very disappointed that I was refused a visa to travel to the US, especially at my failure to answer a simple law question at the interview. However, I stopped beating myself up about it and took up employment at a law firm to gain some experience. I also trusted God had a better plan for me. It is interesting that I met my wife at a reception at another law firm where I went to borrow a law book from my friend to prepare for a court case allocated to me by my senior.

Defeats and failures never have to be the end. They may in fact be the beginning if you respond to the grace of God and learn from your mistakes and failures. Losing one battle does not mean you have lost the war. The real losers and failures in life are those who are 'knocked down' and choose to stay down.

Biblical Heroes who overcame their Failures

It is clear from the Bible that most of the people who made history have failed at some point. These great men include Joshua, Samson, David, Peter and Paul, and their lives demonstrated that with faith it is possible to be even stronger after failure. Their failure and repentance granted them abundant grace of God. They learned from their failures and also learned to know God of a second, third, and fourth chance.

Joshua

I've spoken about Joshua a few times already in this book; he was one of the ten spies selected by Moses on a mission to explore the Promised Land. He was a fearless warrior. He had military expertise and led the Israelites in many successful military expeditions. After Moses' death, he was chosen by God to lead the people of Israel to the Promised Land - Canaan. Under his leadership, the Israelites conquered Canaanites and gained control of the Promised Land. By following God's instruction, he led the destruction of Jericho, the first city to be conquered. After the destruction of Jericho, he led the Israelites to attack Ai, a small neighbouring city to the west. He decided to attack Ai with only a few thousand soldiers. Obviously, he underestimated their opponents' strength. Sadly, they were defeated and 66 Israelites lost their lives. Devastated by the defeat, Joshua cried out to God for help. God heard his cry and told him the cause of the defeat; there was sin in the camp of the Israelites.

God gave Joshua practical instructions; he was to rid Israel of the one who had taken the devoted things, Achan and his household. Joshua obeyed. Joshua learnt his lesson, dealt with the sin in the camp of Israel according to God's instructions. Joshua was instructed by God to attack Ai a second time. This time he was to take all the fighting men. God assured him of victory. Now, because Joshua and the Israelites were rightly related to God, He helped them. They defeated Ai. Their place of defeat was turned to a place of victory. Joshua gained immeasurable wisdom from their initial failure and eventual defeat of Ai. Firstly, he had a deeper awareness of their vulnerability – sin; and a sharper understanding of military logistics necessary to overcome a formidable opponent. When the Israelites repented and put their new insights into action, they became successful at a place of previous failure and defeat.

Like Joshua and the Israelites. You too can turn your place of defeat into a place of victory. God will help you. He desperately wants to help you turn the places of your failure, defeats, losses, humiliation, shame and ridicule to places of success and victory, restoration, strength, honour and dignity. Yes He will, if you trust him and if you are willing to learn from your failures and mistakes.

Samson

Samson was set apart by God to be used to deliver Israel from their enemies. As part of his Nazarite vow, his hair was never to be cut. Unfortunately, he fell in love with Delilah, and she conspired with the enemies who were seeking the source of his unusual and supernatural strength. The Philistine leaders offered her money to help them find out the secret. Using her seductive and deceptive power, Delilah pestered Samson until he told her the secret of his strength. He told her that he was set apart as a Nazarite to God at birth and his hair was never to be cut, otherwise he would lose his supernatural strength. When she realised that Samson had divulged the secret, she made Samson sleep on her lap and quickly called in an aid to shave off the seven braids of his hair. Alas, Samson was drained of his strength and captured by the Philistines. They gouged out his eyes, made him a public spectacle and put him in a prison in Gaza where he was made to grind grain.

Samson sat in the prison, blind and zapped of strength. He felt like a failure. He was humiliated, tortured and lonely. However, he humbled himself and prayed to God for mercy and strength. God answered his prayers and restored his supernatural strength. One day, the Philistines made a great feast to celebrate their victory over Samson. They gathered in a large hall and paraded Samson in the temple to entertain the jeering crowds. Samson wisely asked a young boy to guide him to the pillars of the temple so that he may lean and rest for some time. The boy obeyed. Samson had a plan. He braced himself between the two central pillars of the temple and pushed with all his might, pulling down the building. He killed everyone in the temple, including himself. Although Samson also died when the roof of the temple collapsed, the Bible records that he destroyed more of his enemies at the time of his death than he previously did in his lifetime. Samson experienced failure, humiliation and even lost his life, however, he was not a failure. Interestingly, in Hebrew Chapter 11, the Bible mentioned his name as a hero of faith along with Moses, Abraham and others who were attributed to have *"conquered kingdoms through faith, administered justice and whose weakness was turned to strength".*

I am convinced that it was Samson's faith during his time of failure that earned him an honourable mention in the New Testament. Although Samson's life and experience warns us of the high cost of sin, his faith and dependence on God despite failure can be encouragement that with faith and dependence on God, it is possible to be stronger and victorious despite failures and setbacks.

Fredrick Robertson, a nineteen century British Bible teacher and pastor made an amazing statement in a sermon he preached on August 12, 1849. He stated "Life, like war, is a series of mistakes, and he is not the best Christian or the best general who make the fewest false steps. Poor mediocrity may secure that; but he is the best who wins the most splendid victories, by retrieval of mistakes, forget mistakes, organise victories out of mistakes."

Have you failed in life or feel you are a failure? No matter how bad or how many times you have failed, if you humble yourself and turn over your dependence on God, He will help you. Your failure can make you wiser, smarter and stronger if you have the right attitude, if you do not surrender to failure, or let failure take over your life.

How to Bounce Back from Failure

Here are some strategies that can help you deal with failure:

➢ Don't label yourself as a failure

Resist the temptation of seeing yourself as a failure when you experience the inevitable failure or setbacks. Many people are quick to put the tag 'failure' on themselves the moment they fail at the first, second or third attempt. They see themselves as stupid, dumb and weak. They wallow in defeat and self-pity and close their minds to any possibilities of success. People who internalise failure cannot see beyond their failures. Indeed failures and setbacks are realities of life. All humans fail. You are not the only one who has failed and will not be the last.

➢ Motivate yourself

Often, the biggest problem people have is how to motivate themselves after failure. Getting back up after a fall can be tough, especially when there is no one around to lift you up. Sometimes people around may not be willing to give a helping hand. Many lose hope and give up on their dreams, goals, desires and pursuits the moment they fail or experience setbacks. Some stay down for prolonged periods of time wishing or waiting for someone to come to their aid. Few people know how to become motivated again and rise up after falling. The ability to motivate yourself to rise up and try again after failure, setbacks and defeat is an essential survival skill in your life.

To get motivated after failure, it is important you accept the reality of failure. Do not dwell on your failures or make failure personal. Failure happens to us all! If you focus on your failure or continually internalise failure, you will stay discouraged and ultimately become a prisoner to failure. Instead of focusing on your failure, remind yourself of your past successes, accomplishments and victories whether big or small. Your past successes and accomplishments are proof that you are not a failure.

You have the ability within you to accomplish almost any goal, project or vision that you set for yourself. When I was a young child, I read the story of '*The Little*

Engine That Could' in an illustrated children's book first published in the US in 1930 by Platt & Munk. The story is used to teach children the value of optimism and hard work.

"A little railroad engine was employed about a station yard for such work as it was built for – pulling a few cars on and off the switches. One morning it was waiting for the next call when a long train of freight cars asked a large engine in the round house to take it over the hill. "I can't, that is too much a pull for me" said the great engine built for hard work. Then the train asked another engine, and another, only to hear excuses and be refused. In desperation, the train asked the little switch engine to draw it up the grade and down on the other side. "I think I can" puffed the little locomotive, and put itself in front of the great heavy train. As it went on the little engine kept bravely puffing faster and faster, "I think I can, I think I can, I think I can". As it neared the top of the grade which had so discouraged the larger engines, it went more slowly. However, it kept saying, "I – think - I can, I – think - I can". It reached the top by drawing on bravery and then went on down the grade, congratulating itself by saying, "I thought I could, I thought I could."

If you think you can, you will. Start telling yourself you can. You can bounce back after failure, you can overcome your setbacks, you can move beyond your limits. Yes, you can move mountains, you can achieve extraordinary success. Yes, you can!

➤   Find out what went wrong

I wrote earlier on that following the first experience of defeat of the Israelites in the hands of Ai, Joshua sought God for the reason for the defeat. Anytime you fail, try to find the reason for the failure. Analyse the situation. Find out what went wrong. Look for lessons to learn so that you don't repeat the same mistakes. Consider any knowledge, information, experience or skills that may be lacking and how to acquire them. Think of how to achieve a better outcome next time you attempt the same problem.

➤ Learn

John Dewey said "Failure is instructive, the person who really thinks learns quite as much from his failures as from his success". Walter Brunell also observed that "Failure is the tuition you pay for success."

It is often said that "Attitude determines altitude". Have a positive attitude about failure. See failure as a teacher and take advantage of the opportunity to learn. Every failure teaches you something. Improve and polish your skills. If you have the right attitude you will learn a lot from your failures, you learn about yourself, about others, and about life. Following your failure, you may learn to improve and polish your skills.

➤ Develop a better plan

One of the reasons for failure is the lack of planning, or poor or unrealistic plans. All successful people carefully plan and detail how they intend to achieve their objectives. It's important you develop a plan on how you intend to achieve your dreams and goals. Careful and thorough planning will help you identify any potential problems, obstacles, needs, weakness, strengths and opportunities. Planning will help you focus your time, energy and resources on achieving your goals and objectives

Take time to plan your actions, strategies, resources, potential problems and solutions. I often ask people if they have a written plan about how they intend to achieve their dreams and objectives. It is interesting that many people do not have a written plan. Write down your plan. Never trust your mind to remember it all. Your plan will not be perfect the first time you create it. However, you can revisit, correct or even re-create it based on new information, resources, opportunities, challenges and setbacks.

➤   Try again

Babies and toddlers are like little wonders. They amuse me with their learning skills, resilience and persistence.

Watching a baby learn to walk is very interesting. They stumble and fall, they try again, fall again, but keep on trying until they are able to walk properly. Our first son, Emmanuel, probably fell a thousand times a day when he was learning to walk. My wife used to be very upset whenever he fell, especially with the bumps and bruises that developed on his body. Despite the falls, Emmanuel would not give up trying his walking adventure. Sometimes he walked awkwardly but kept on trying; gaining more confidence and balance each time he tried.

I believe we all have so much to learn from these little wonders. We can rise up after every fall and failure and keep on trying until we succeed. If babies can sum up courage, despite several falls and get back in their attempt to walk and have mastery over failures, you can, I can, everyone can if we keep on trying and don't give up.

Successful people know how to develop success from failures. They persistently try again and even many times until they eventually achieve their dreams and objectives.

After JK Rowling finished her manuscript for *Harry Potter and the Philosopher's Stone* on an old manual typewriter, twelve publishers rejected her manuscript. She kept trying to find a publisher who would be willing to publish the book. Eventually Barry Cunningham, an editor at Bloomsbury (a publishing house in London) agreed to publish the book. He advised her however, to get a day's job as he thought she had little chance of making money with a children's book.

In 1997, Bloomsbury published Philosopher's Stone with an initial print run of 1,000 copies, 500 of which were distributed to libraries. Later in the year, the book won its first award, Nestle Smarties Book Prize. In February 1998, the novel won the British Book Award for Children's Books of the Year. In October 1998, Scholastic Inc, a US publishing company, published the book under the tittle *Harry Potter and the Sorcerer's Stone*. The rest is history, as they say. JK Rowling went on to write and publish seven series of Harry Potter all of which became bestsellers. Harry Potter is now a global brand worth an estimated $15 billion. The series, which total 4,195 pages, have been translated, in whole or in part, into 67 languages.

I can imagine, she would have been discouraged after the initial rejections of the manuscript in 1995. What would have happened if she stopped trying to find a publisher after the first few rejections? Supposing she abandoned her dream when the eleventh or twelfth publishing company rejected her manuscript? Many people have abandoned their dreams, hope and aspirations at the edge of their breakthrough because of setbacks and temporary defeats. Don't be among those who abandon their dreams and goals. Try again. Keep trying until you succeed.

CHAPTER NINE

THE POWER OF PERSISTENCE

On my first day out in January this year, I decided to use public transport to my office rather than travelling by car. In the train I picked up a newspaper left on one of the seats. It was unusual for me to read newspapers in the early hours of the day. I would normally read inspirational and faith-filled books or write in my personal journal. An article in the newspaper titled 'The Essence of a Fighting Spirit' caught my attention. The author described a show that portrayed the importance of fighting our limits and how we should try to keep going even when our world changes. Even when your world changes, you can still fight for the victory! I wondered how we can fight our limits, though our world seems to be turning upside down, when we encounter roadblocks and setbacks. It takes persistence.

Persistence is the ability to keep moving forward, pushing on, fighting on, regardless of limitations, challenges and setbacks. Persistence will give you everything. It will give you mental strength and help shape your character. Persistence will make you a winner and a conqueror. Persistence will help you break barriers, move you beyond your limits and help you turn stumbling blocks into stepping stones.

I once read about qualities of a good boxer in an article titled 'The Beginning of Boxing History'. The article refers to the six manuals on Olympic training by a Greek philosopher and sports enthusiast, Flavius Philostratus, where he describes a good boxer as "one with long, powerful arms, strong shoulders, a high neck, and powerful, flexible body. According to the author, a good boxer must also possess persistence, patience, endurance, great will-power and strength. He asserts that without these qualities, a boxer cannot climb to the pinnacle of the sport.

The achievers in this world are true fighters. They never quit or give up on their dreams. They harness the unstoppable power of persistence to push beyond their limits, despite adversity and setbacks. Persistence is the fuel that keeps them going against all odds and apparent defeats.

Björn Borg, a tennis ace and Wimbledon legend once said "My greatest point is my persistence. I never give up in a match. However down I am, I fight until the last ball. My lists of matches show that I have turned a great many 'so called' irretrievable defeats into victory". Yes, you can too. With persistence and determination, you too can pass through the hurdles of challenges, discouragements and uncertainty to attain your goals, dreams and aspirations.

In his poem "*Don't Quit*", Edgar Albert Guest gave a powerful word of encouragement for us to forge ahead even when the going gets tough. This is what he wrote:

"*When things go wrong, as they sometimes will,*
When the road you're trudging seems all uphill,
When the funds are low and the debts are high,
And you want to smile, but you have to sigh,
When care is pressing you down a bit
Rest if you must, but don't you quit.

Life is queer with its twists and its turns,
As every one of us sometimes learns,
And many a failure turns about
When they might have won, had they stuck it out.
Don't give up though the pace seems slow,
You may succeed with another blow.
Often the struggler has given up
When he might have captured the victor's cup;
And he learned too late when the night came down,
How close he was to the golden crown.
Success is failure turned inside out
The silver tint of the clouds of doubt
And you never can tell how close you are,
It may be near when it seems so far;
So stick to the fight when you're hardest hit,
It's when things seem worst that you must not quit!"

Sylvester Stallone, an American actor, screen writer and film director, has a very fascinating story. As a young man, he aspired to be a movie star. However, he could not find a talent agency willing to take him on. He struggled to pay his household bills or meet up with his obligations. He was under constant pressure from his wife to give up his dream and get a job.

Sylvester watched a boxing match on TV between Muhammad Ali and Chuck Wepner. Despite being slaughtered by Ali, Wepner kept holding his ground and coming back for more. He was an underdog but kept fighting despite the slim chance he would even get close to winning. This inspired Stallone to begin writing the script for the movie 'Rocky'. He wrote for over 24 hours straight and completed the entire script. He tried to sell the screenplay to many producers but was rejected many times. Eventually someone loved it and agreed to do the movie. He told them that he wanted to play the starring part. They declined and told him he was a writer not an actor. Stallone disagreed and told them he was an actor. He declined their offer of over $100,000 despite his current financial situation. He was offered even more money, as long as he agreed not to act in the movie, but he declined again. The offer kept rising just so he would sell them the film without playing the part. The price eventually got to around $400,000 but he stood his ground. Eventually they offered Stallone $25,000 and the lead role in the movie, which he finally accepted. The rest is history. 'Rocky' won the Academy Award for Best Picture in 1976.

Sylvester Stallone achieved his dream. He believed in himself and his dream. He never gave up. He kept trying and trying until he finally made it. You too can achieve your dream against all odds. With persistence, you can overcome all the obstacles.

The popular singer, Steve Wonder, was born four months premature and had to be put in an incubator, a man-made womb. Due to too much oxygen while inside the incubator, Stevie's eyesight was destroyed.

When Stevie was two years of age he showed an interest in music. He would always listen to the radio and even create his own music by using spoons to bang on pots and pans. At the age of four, Stevie was already playing the harmonica and the piano. He attended Michigan's School for the Blind. He said "People at school told me I couldn't make it, that I'd end up making potholders instead. But after I thought I wanted to be a musician, I became determined simply to prove those people wrong." Stevie sang in a local church choir and soon after became the church soloist when he was nine. After being caught singing rock and roll, Stevie was expelled from the choir. However Stevie continued pursing his dream of becoming a singer.

In 1963, at the age of thirteen, Stevie's Wonder's first recording was a hit. It sold over one million copies and topped the charts for fifteen weeks. The name of the recording was 'Fingertips. Stevie Wonder's singing career has been remarkable not just for his musical genius, but for his persistence in overcoming obstacles - most notably his blindness. He was awarded the Grammy's Lifetime Achievement Award in 1996 and was inducted into the Rock and Roll Hall of Fame in 1989.

Nelson Mandela was a champion of principle. He had a goal: to end apartheid, and would stop at nothing until it was achieved. In 1963, he was arrested for terrorism and treason and sentenced to life in prison.

Whilst in prison, Mandela continued his fight for equal rights for all South Africans; not just non-whites. He refused to compromise his political beliefs for freedom and persisted at fighting for the end of apartheid. His persistence paid off and he was released after twenty-seven years. At the age of 75 (four years later), he won the first ever free and fair election in South Africa – finally obtaining what he had spent most of his life fighting for: equal rights for all races and a democratic state. He fought for what he believed in and left a legacy for the entire world.

Peter J Daniels said "We should never shut up, give up, until God takes us up." By this he simply means we should not give up on our dreams no matter the obstacles or how many times we fail.

In Luke 18, Jesus tells a parable of a widow in order to teach about importance of persistence in prayer.

The widow had an unresolved legal issue with an adversary. She apparently lacked family support and the finances to hire an attorney – she was desperate. Out of her desperation, she persistently appealed for justice from an ungodly judge who neither feared God nor cared about people. But because of the widow's persistence he finally relented and gave the widow that - justice.

A blind man named Bartimaeus was begging on the side of a road. He had heard about the miraculous power of Jesus Christ. When he heard that Jesus was passing by he began to shout *"Jesus, son of David, have mercy on me".* People nearby rebuked him and told him to be quiet, but he shouted all the more, *"Son of David, have mercy on me!"* Bartimaeus was determined to do his best to get Jesus' attention. He ignored those who told him to be quiet, hoping that Jesus would notice him. His persistence and determination paid off and he got Jesus' attention. Jesus stopped and told his disciples to call him. When he got to him, Jesus asked him what he wanted him to do for him. The blind man was clear about what he wanted. He responded *"Rabbi, I want to see".*

Jesus said to him "Go, *your faith has healed you."* Immediately he received his sight. Persistence will hand you your desired miracle.

A young man was embarking on a journey. He was very excited at the start of the journey as he had seen people who successfully completed the journey and had heard stories about the good life on the other side. He encountered obstacles along the way, was tired, discouraged and reasoned it was better for him to go back or at least camp where he was. As he was considering about giving up, a stranger appeared to him. He looked strong and built. "Who are you?" the traveller asked.

"My name is Persistence. I am the backbone of all great achievements. I am the fire that burns in the hearts of great achievers. I am able to pull down barriers. If you allow me, I will stretch you beyond the limitation of your mind and circumstances. I have the power that can enlist your name in the hall of fame."

"Many people in the journey of life have fallen short of their dreams and aspirations because they quit in the middle of their journey. They allowed their fears and doubts to paralyse them from moving towards their goals and aspirations. They could not withstand the storms of hardships, discomfort and uncertainty." He continued "It grieves my heart when I see would-be great men and women, young and old, give up on their dreams and settle for less. They settled for much less than what they could accomplish or be". They did not endure the discipline of persistence and therefore unable to taste the joy of accomplishments.

The traveller noticed a golden key in his hand and asked, "What is that?"

"I hold the key to success. If you persist I will hand over the key to you", Persistence answered.

As they continued the conversation, the traveller noticed another stranger standing next to them. He also looked strong and powerful. He looked determined and confident. He waited for Persistence to conclude his statement before introducing himself.

"My name is Determination. Persistence and I are brothers. We help achievers along the way. We help them turn the impossible into the possible. Only the determined can achieve their goals. The weak and double minded cannot. They give up easily. I am the voice of wisdom that speaks to men. I help strengthen their resolve against all odds."

Friend, I hope you will embrace persistence and determination. Nothing can stand in their way and nothing can stand in your way if you persist.

John the Baptist, the forerunner of Jesus Christ described himself as the "Voice of Him that cries in the wilderness". His mission was to prepare the way for the coming of Christ the Messiah.

Persistence is like the ministry of John the Baptist, working to prepare the way for your victory, successes, breakthroughs and achievements. It's the voice that tells you to try again. It's the energy that fuels your ambition when all odds are against you.

The Bible states in Luke 1:80 that John the Baptism was in the wilderness and getting strong in the spirit until his manifestation to Israel. Persistence is that force that strengthens you, pushes you forward in the wilderness of solitude and difficulties until the manifestation of your dreams. Persistence will not just give you the key to success, it will also give you the opportunity to grow, develop and stretch your spiritual, mental, emotional, and physical capability.

Ralph Waldo Emerson, a former American essayist and poet, said "That which we persist in doing becomes easier to do, not that the nature of the thing has changed, but that our power to do it has increased."

Sir Edward Hillary, New Zealand born mountaineer, set his sights on Everest, the world highest mountain. In 1952, he failed in his attempt to reach the top of the mountain. However, the British parliament decided to honour him with an award. When he entered the chamber to receive his award he saw a large picture of Everest set up at the corner of the chamber. During the standing ovation as he walked into the room, walked over to the picture, shook his fist at it and screamed at the mountain: "You defeated me. But you won't defeat me again! Because you have grown all that you can, but I am still growing!"

True to his words, he and his expedition partner, Nepalese Tenzing Norgay reached the top of Mount Everest, 29,000 feet, at 11.30am on the 29th May 1953. They were the first explorers to reach the summit of Mount Everest. With persistence and determination he conquered Everest!

You may be wondering how you can develop persistence. You already have the capacity. The Bible states that God has put in all of us a measure of faith. However, it's important you decide what you want to achieve. You need to have a clear vision of what you want to achieve. This includes identifying your desires, hopes and aspirations. Napoleon Hill in his book *'Master Keys to Riches'* states "The starting point to individual achievement is the adoption of a definite purpose and definite plan for its attainment."

Paul the Apostle had a clear vision of Christ and he was determined to preach Christ. The clarity of his goal was affirmed when he stated in 1st Corinthians 1:17 that *"Christ has not sent him to baptise, but to preach the gospel"*. This clarity of vision enabled him to focus and persevere despite persecutions and obstacles. In 1st Corinthians 9:26, he stated *"I do not run like a man running aimlessly, I do not fight like a boxer beating the air".*

Your goals should be exciting, capable of bringing positive benefits to you and others. All great achievers see beyond the present, they saw beyond their challenges, obstacles and temporary defeats. They saw the benefits and beneficiaries of their dreams and visions.

The Bible states in Hebrews Chapter 12 verse 2 that Jesus endured the cross for the joy set before him.

He saw beyond His sufferings

He saw beyond the cross
He saw multitudes of people delivered
He saw multitudes freed
He saw multitudes saved

Dr Martin Luther King saw a different America where people were no longer judged by the colour of their skin. In his speech in Memphis on the 3rd April 1963, the day before he was assassinated, he boldly declared: "I've looked over, and I've seen the Promised Land. I may not get there with you, but I want you to know tonight that we as a people will get to the Promised Land".

Joseph saw beyond his captivity, he saw beyond the confines of the prison. He saw the sun, moon and eleven stars bowing to him. This gave him the grace to endure and persist in his integrity and trust in God in the face of adversity.

What is your motivation, reason for your goals and pursuit? This will give you energy and the reason to endure. Apostle Paul stated in 2nd Timothy 2:10 *"I endure all things for the elect sake"*.

It's amazing what mothers will go through for their children. About two years ago, I read the news about a determined mum who endured labour for seventy five days to ensure the safe delivery of her babies. She was pregnant with triplets, but lost one of the babies when she went into labour prematurely. The doctors decided that she needed to reduce the pressure of gravity on her cervix to prevent more premature births, so they came up with the idea of her lying nearly upside down to try to ease her contractions and prolong the labour to increase the babies' chances of surviving. She remained in that awkward position for two and half months until the two babies were delivered safely.

When the woman was interviewed by a news agency about how she was able to endure such an awkward position for so long, she stated that the prospect of lying upside down for weeks did not bother her as she was more concerned about saving her babies.

What a motivation! Her bravery is commendable. I wish I had the chance to meet her and present her with lovely flowers!

Og Mandino wrote motivating messages about the power of persistence. This time tested wisdom is contained in scroll marked 111 in his famous book '*The Greatest Salesman in the World*'. You will find the message inspiring and motivating. In the book, he talks about how young bulls were tested. Each bull would be brought into the ring and allowed to attack the picador who would prick them with a lance. The bravery of each bull was rated by how many times the bull kept charging in spite of the sting of the blade.

Do you realise that each day we are tested by life in a similar way? We all face obstacles, challenges and feel the stings of life. However, it is those who continue to charge forward, who succeed. Will you continue to try and charge forward despite the pain and setbacks until you succeed? Will you continue the race until you reach the finish line? Will you endure until the end?

Friend, if you persist you will win. Yes, you will win. You will succeed. Harness the unstoppable power of persistence. With persistence you will succeed. Be someone who persists no matter what the situation or challenge may be. Make up your mind that you are not going to give up.

Trust God to help you. Yes, He will help you. He will strengthen and uphold you.

CHAPTER TEN

SEIZE YOUR MOMENTS

A few years ago, I was watching a football match between two local African clubs; the Alliance team and Eagles team. The Alliance team had so many chances to score, especially in the first half. As early as in the first minute, a chance was missed and in the first ten minutes of the second half, open goals were kicked over the bar! It was a match full of missed chances as well as a missed penalty kick at a crucial moment in the 85th minute. Despite having seven corner kicks and two penalty kicks to their advantage, Alliance could not convert their opportunities into goals.

Sixty-five minutes into the game, one of the Eagles strikers picked up a loose ball in the opponents half and fired the ball into the corner of the net. Ten minutes later, a corner kick in favour of the Eagles led to another striker heading the ball into the net. The game ended with Alliance team losing and reflecting how different the outcome could have been if they had seized their moments of opportunities. The Eagles were not better than the Alliance team, however, they took advantage of the opportunities they had and therefore won the match.

Life is all about moments. When an opportunity presents itself, do you seize the moment and grab it or do you let the moment pass? If you do not seize your moments of opportunity, they will pass.

The story of Bartimaeus in Mark 10 is inspirational. He was blind and poor. He could only survive by begging for alms on the roadside. However, he recognised his moment of miracle and seized his opportunity. He did not allow the moment to pass by. He refused to allow the negative voices around him to quieten him. He knew it was his moment: his moment of change, of new beginnings, and of fulfilled dreams. He seized his moment and his life did not remain the same.

Friend, you too can make the most of opportunities that God brings your way if you reject the negative voices of your failures, defeats, unbelief, doubts, condemnation, fear, discouragement and intimidation around you. You too can experience your desired change and transformation if you recognise your moments of opportunity and act on them. Do not stay by the roadside blinded by challenges that life had thrown at you. Rise up, seize your moment! Make it your moment of restoration and new beginnings.

Goliath the champion of the Philistines was nine feet, four inches tall. He had a solid bronze helmet, a bronze coat that weighed 125 pounds and bronze shin guards. He had a bronze javelin that was the size of a weaver's beam with a 15-pound iron spearhead. His size, coupled with his amour and a personal shield bearer, made the Israelites soldiers terrified. All of the Israelites army was dreadfully afraid of him. There was no one among them who would take on Goliath. Every one fled from him whenever he came forward to challenge the Israelites.

When David got to the battlefield and heard Goliath shouting his daily defiance, he saw fear stirred within the army of Israel. One of the soldiers mentioned to David that the King had offered huge reward to anyone who could defeat Goliath. The King had offered that whoever defeat Goliath "would be greatly enriched by the King, he would get to marry the King's daughter and his family would be granted tax exemption".

David could hardly believe his ears when he heard about the rewards. He must have thought "This sounds interesting. This is my moment, I'll go for it. I know the Lord will grant me success". David recognised his moment of opportunity and was willing to take the risk. Although his oldest brother Eliab misunderstood his intention and tried to intimidate David by saying *"Why did you come down here? Who is watching those few sheep for you in the wilderness? I know how arrogant you are and your devious plan: you came down just to see the battle!* "David ignored his brother and turned to another Israelite soldier to ascertain the rewards the King had offered for whoever defeats Goliath. Despite the frightening sight of Goliath and intimidation from his brother, David volunteered to fight Goliath. It took some persuasion, but King Saul finally agreed to let David fight against the giant.

Dressed in his simple tunic, carrying his shepherd's staff, sling and a pouch full of stones, David hurried and ran toward Goliath. He put his hand in his bag and took out a stone and slung it and struck Goliath in his forehead and he fell on his face to the earth. While the Israelites army were paralysed by fear at the sight of Goliath, David confronted his fear, stepped out in faith and seized his moment of divine opportunity. David gained fame with his defeat of Goliath and gained a position in the army, becoming a leader of the Israelites army in addition to the rewards promised by the King.

Fear is one of the greatest barriers to opportunities. Many people are in the habit of seeing the negative side of any challenging situation. If you focus more on how big your challenge seems, you can miss your moment of opportunity. The more you focus on how big your challenges and obstacles are, the more fear will grip your heart and you will be blind to opportunity when it presents itself. Don't allow your fears to hinder you. You can confront your fears, but you may need to change your perspective.

I once heard a story of a wise, little boy who tried to change his perspective. There was a big bully down the street who was always bothering the little boy. The boy tried to summon up the courage so he could stand up to the bully, but he was still too afraid. One day, his father bought him a telescope. The boy was out in the front yard playing with his new telescope, but he was looking through the wrong end. He was looking through the big end instead of the small. His father noticed this and stepped outside and said "No son, you are doing it backward. Turn it around and it will make everything bigger like it was meant to do." The little boy said" I know Dad, but right now I'm looking at this bully. When I look at him this way, it makes him so small that I'm not afraid of him anymore".

Like that little boy, you too may need to turn your telescope, your perspective, your thoughts, and your attitudes around so you can see your problems and situation differently. If you turn it around, you will see your situation from a divine perspective – God's. You'll see from the perspective of faith instead of fear. You'll be able to recognise opportunities, overcome your fears and seize your moments.

You don't have to be completely fearless before taking action to seize your moments of opportunity. Successful people take action despite their fears and feelings of uncertainty.

Esther knew that even as Queen she could only go to the King if summoned. Anyone who simply showed up in the throne room was subject to death. Only if the King lifted his sceptre and allowed her to enter would her life be spared. She was frightened. Despite her fears, she gathered her strength and courage, fortified herself by fasting and prayers and appeared before the King. In the end, her actions saved her people.

Taking a driving test can be a stressful and terrifying experience. I had expected to pass my driving test in UK the first time, but I failed with three minor mistakes and one major: I did not stop at a major roundabout. I booked the second test one month later. Although I had practiced and was confident that I was able to execute all the driving manoeuvres and routines that I could be tested on, considering my first failure, I was nervous in the beginning. Despite my fears, I was determined to go for it. I calmed myself down and kept both hands on the wheel. At the end of the test the examiner said "Congratulations, you have passed!" It was a terrific feeling. I felt proud of myself for fighting through my fears. I wondered what the result would have been if I had allowed my fears to overcome me. I would have missed my golden opportunity. Your fears are completely dependent on you for their survival. You may feel afraid, but if you confront your fear with courage and determination, you will achieve your dreams, desires and aspirations.

Moments of Solitude

The account of Jacob wrestling with an angel of God in Genesis 32 is well known among Christians.

After 20 years in exile, Jacob decided to return to his homeland. However, he became afraid when he learnt that his brother Esau was on his way to meet him. Years ago, he had tricked his brother Esau and his father Isaac to obtain the blessing of the first son. Esau was very bitter and intended to kill him. Jacob had to flee their homeland to the far away land of Haran to escape his brother's wrath. During his years in exile, he got married, had children and great possession of livestock, especially sheep and cattle.

Now after many years of being apart Jacob had to face his brother. Thoughts about the past bombarded his mind. Will Esau carry out his threats to kill him? What will become of his precious family? Had Esau forgiven him? What can he do to appease his brother? Jacob's mind could not rest. Although Jacob had changed and matured in character over the years, he was not sure if his brother was still seeking revenge. Hoping to make amends, he sent ahead gifts to his brother Esau.

The night before the two brothers were to meet, Jacob, sent his family across the ford river while he alone remained behind. He decided to spend the last night alone in prayers to God. He was without his family, and possessions. In that moment, he separated himself from all that made life dear to him. He was alone.

In Genesis 32 verse 24, the Bible states *"So Jacob was left alone, and a man wrestled with him till day break.* While there alone in the darkness he was assaulted by an unknown man. But the stranger was not a mere man. He was an angel of God.

Somehow, Jacob recognised that his opponent was a divine messenger who had the power to bless him. When the angel saw that he could not prevail against Jacob, he touched his thigh. Immediately the thigh came out of joint. Despite his physical pains, Jacob held on to the angel. At some point the angel said to

Jacob *"Let me go, for the day has broken."* However, Jacob responded *"I will not let you go unless you bless me".*

"What is your name?" the angel inquired.

He responded *"Jacob"*

The angel then declared *"Your name shall no longer be called Jacob, but Israel, for you have striven with God and with men, and have prevailed."*

Jacob seized his divine moment and his life was changed forever. The Lord heard his prayer and changed the heart of his brother Esau.

Life-changing things happen in our moments of solitude, moments when we are alone. God often meets us in those moments of solitude when we wrestle with our fears, our failures, our rejections, our pains, our losses, our inadequacies, our emptiness, our loneliness, our past or present challenges, and uncertainty of future. Your most significant moments can be moments when you are alone with God or even by yourself.

The Bible records numerous times when Jesus withdrew to lonely places to pray and meditate. He knew it was important for Him to regularly withdraw from distractions and pressures of the world around Him to focus His attention solely on God.

At the beginning of His ministry, he withdrew to the wilderness and spends 40 days alone praying and fasting. At the end of His fasting, He was tempted by the Devil, but He overcame the temptation as recorded in the Bible in Matthew 4. In Luke 6:12-13, the Bible records that Jesus went out to a mountainside to pray, and spent the night praying to God. When morning came, He called His disciples to Him and chose twelve of them, whom He also designated apostles. After He miraculously fed 5,000, He also withdrew to be alone with God. Jesus knew the purpose for which He had come to the earth was to give His life as a ransom to many. He knew He would soon be arrested, falsely accused and executed. He took a group of His disciples and went to the garden of Gethsemane to pray. At some point He was alone praying to God about His impending suffering and death.

Setting aside time to be alone with God will deepen your relationship with Him. In Matthew 6:6, Jesus told His disciples *"When you pray, go away by yourself, shut the door behind you, and pray to your Father secretly. Then your Father, who knows all secrets, will reward you."*

When you make the effort to get alone with God, prayerfully focusing your attention solely on Him, He will reward you with blessings that you may not receive any other way.

In Samuel Chapter 1, the Bible reveals the story of a woman named Hannah who was barren, and desperately needed a child. Hannah was one of the two wives of a man named Elkanah who lived in the hill country of Ephraim. Polygamy was never an ideal situation. The practice was far from the standard of monogamy set out by God in the Garden of Eden between Adam and Eve. Rivalry, strife and heartaches were all too common in polygamous families.

The other wife of Elkanah, Peninnah, had children, but Hannah had no child. She desired a child, however, she could not conceive. Hannah was very disheartened because of her childlessness. To make matters worse, Peninnah taunted her concerning her barrenness. Although Elkanah loved Hannah and was kind to her, Hannah could not bear the pain of Peninnah's taunting and unkindness. She desperately desired a child.

Every year the family went to Shiloh to worship. On one of those yearly trips, Hannah pulled away from the group and went into the tabernacle by herself to be alone with God. She seized the moment to pour her heart to God. She prayed and asked God to give her a son. She was keen not only to receive a blessing from God, but also to give to God. So she made a vow to God that if she had a son, she would dedicate the child to a life of service to God. After pouring her heart to God, she was a changed person. She had transferred the weight of her emotional burden to the Lord. She knew in her heart that the Lord was going to answer her prayer.

The family returned to their home in Ramah and in time Hannah conceived and had a baby boy. She named him Samuel, a name which means "heard by God". Hannah did as she promised, shortly after the child was weaned she gave Samuel up to God's service under the care of Eli, the high priest. God blessed Hannah by giving her more children. She asked for one son, but God gave her five more children!

When you feel overwhelmed, or burdened with the pressures and challenges of life, or overcome with sadness, it may be a time for you to get alone with God and pour your hearts to Him. In Matthew 11:28-30, the Lord Jesus declared *"Come unto me, all ye that labour and are heavy laden, and I will give you rest."*

You might be heavy laden right now. You might be burdened down by the weight of trials and tribulations in your personal life, family, place of work, business, ministry or other community projects. Like Hannah you might be aching under the pressure of inability to have children or even under the pressure of raising children alone. Why not take time to get alone with God pouring your hearts to him? As the Bible encourages in 1 Peter

5 verse 7 *"Cast all your cares upon God, for He cares for you."*

In a world of constant pressure, commitments and demands on time, surrounded by many people and distraction of technology, you need to create time to be alone. I strongly believe that seizing a moment of solitude is a necessity. There you will find true peace and rest for your soul and body.

Many people associate solitude or being alone with feelings of loneliness and isolation. Loneliness is a painful and negative state of mind marked by feelings of emptiness, inadequacy, unimportance and rejection. You may even be surrounded by people and still feel lonely. Solitude is a choice to be alone without feeling lonely. It is a positive state of mind marked by constructive state of engagement with yourself. When you are alone, you enjoy being in your own company, connect to your soul, interests, nature and do things that interest you.

Benefits of Solitude

Being around family, friends, colleagues, associates, customers and other groups that we are connected with is great. Relationships with people are very important aspects of life that have a positive impact in our lives. However, finding time to be alone has a lot of benefits.

It is often when we are alone that we are able to reach inside ourselves and find truth, strength, courage and uniqueness. In your solitary moments, you will become more acquitted with yourself, your interests, your passions and dreams. Solitude allows you to put off your problems and tasks momentarily and focus on yourself.

Solitude can help your concentration. Time alone can help clear your mind of clutter, remove distractions and help you focus.

Being alone can be a time of rest and refreshment for your soul and body. In addition to your normal sleep, solitude gives you the opportunity to relax and disconnect from constant issues that bombard your mind. It provides you the much needed break that can ease stress and burnout. Richard Mahler, a writer based in New Mexico and media consultant, in his book *'Stillness: Daily Gifts of Solitude'* states "if we could package and sell solitude as an antidote for stress and dysfunction the tide would turn".

Your quiet moments are not just restoratives. They are also potential creative moments. Solitude enhances creativity. Most of the greatest artistic and inventions were born in the place of solitude and quietness. History is filled with great men and women who have testified to the value of solitude.

Thomas Edison, the popular American inventor who developed phonograph, the motion picture camera and the light bulb observed that "the best thinking has been done in solitude".

Albert Einstein, a German-born theoretical physicist who developed the general theory of relativity, said "the monotony and solitude of a quiet life stimulates the creative mind".

Nikola Tesla, a Serbian-American engineer, inventor and physicist who contributed to the invention of electromagnetic devices, also observed that "The mind is sharper and keener in seclusion and uninterrupted solitude. Originality thrives in seclusion, free of outside influences beating upon us to cripple the creative mind.

Be alone, that's the secret of invention, be alone that is when ideas are born".

JK Rowling's first idea for Harry Potter started in 1990 when she was travelling alone on a delayed train from Manchester to London. She described how it all started on her official website. She states "I was travelling back to London on my own on a crowded train, and the idea of Harry Potter simply fell into my head. I had been writing almost continuously since the age of six but I had never been so excited about an idea before. To my immense frustration, I didn't have a pen that worked, and I was too shy to ask anybody if I could borrow one. I did not have a functioning pen with me, but I do think that this was probably a good thing. I simply sat and thought, for four hours (delayed train), while all the details bubbled up in my brain, and this scrawny, black- haired, respectable boy who didn't know he was a wizard become more and more real to me".

Amazing! JK Rowling seized her moment on that delayed train. A journey that would have been a disappointment for many on the train turned to be a creative moment for her. While in the solitude of her thoughts, her imaginative genius came alive. An idea that would turn her entire life around started bubbling in her mind.

Riding the creative wave is exciting and exhilarating. Ideas usually come to me in my quiet and solitary moments. Sometimes this is at home in the bath, or when travelling on the bus, train, or on a plane, in the library, and any other time where I have scheduled to be alone. These are times when I receive most of my writing inspirations and other creative ideas. They are my 'aha' moments. My imaginations suddenly become strong and real. Ideas flow in my mind like a river. They are like magical moments to me. Oh I crave for those moments! I really do. I try my best to organise my life and schedules to experience the moments over and over again. I usually have a notepad and pen handy ready to seize the creative waves when they present themselves. They are very empowering and exciting!

You too can experience and ride the creative wave. You can connect to the creative genius inside of you, but you have to be willing to enjoy your own company and make solitude your friend. That's where you reach deep within your soul and draw out a hidden genius locked inside of you that always screaming for freedom of expression.

Whether it is for time alone with God, or for quiet contemplation, intense concentration, creative work, relaxation and restoration, your solitary moments are necessary for your well-being. However, you have to make the choice to put yourself on your own priority list. Let me remind you that you matter so much to God. In Isaiah 49:16, the Bible states that *"God has written your name on the palm of His hands"*. That is how important you are to Him. You are His priority! When He looks at the palm of His hand, He thinks of you, your needs, your well-being, your health, your progress, your future and your destiny. Everything in your life matters to Him. He cares so much about your life. Knowing this, you better remember to put yourself on your priority list.

A few years ago, I used to spend so much of my time on legitimate and noble things that I felt must be done, to the detriment of things that I really loved to do. I allowed the constant demands of people and pressure of responsibilities of life to dictate my days. I was always frustrated with myself. I was always saying "I'm too busy! I don't have time for myself, I wish I could have more time for myself". Thank God I realised that "If wishes were horses, beggars would ride." I decided to re- evaluate my life and priorities and put myself as a priority. This drastically changed my life and I have never regretted the decision. The more time I spend alone, the more courage I find to pursue my dreams and aspirations, and the more time and energy I seem to have.

Finding time for yourself often comes down to you making a conscious decision to carve out this time. Remember that you have only 24 hours in your day. You cannot create more time, but you can clear some time by re-evaluating your priorities.

Here are a few tips that you may consider that can help you set aside more time for yourself.

Mark off time in your day planner, weekly schedule or monthly or yearly calendar to spend time alone.

Peter J Daniels, the Australian businessman and life coach explained one of the secrets of his turnaround from failure to success this way, "I scheduled time to think. In fact, I reserve one day a week on my calendar just to think. All of my greatest ideas, opportunities and money-making ventures started with the days I took off to think. I used to lock myself away in my den with strict instructions to my family that under no circumstances was I to be disturbed".

You may not have the luxury of scheduling a whole day every week to spend by yourself, but you can certainly carve out 15 or 30 minutes, or even an hour to spend each week reflecting on your life, goals, and aspirations, and creating a vision and strategies for a better future for yourself. You'll be amazed by the extra lifts you'll get into your future. You'll be much closer to achieving your goals and dreams faster than you can imagine.

Solitude can be experienced at home, but ensure you close the door to all distractions: telephones, the internet, social media, TV, and magazines. Simply turn off! You may also consider waking up early to spend some time by yourself. This probably can be a good time for quiet time, prayers, Bible study, meditation or reflective thinking.

Go on retreats. Making time to go on retreats is one of the profitable investments in yourself. A retreat will give you the chance to pause and look at your life with a new perspective and unlock answers to questions that you may not have taken time to ask. It can also be a nurturing 'time out' just for you; a time to rejuvenate your mind, body and spirit. In today's fast-paced world, juggling the demands of work, business, ministry, family and your personal life can feel overwhelming. Going on a retreat can be the perfect opportunity you need to restore and keep yourself at the optimum level of wellness. A retreat is also a good place to spend quality time with God. It is a place where you shut the door on the world and open the windows to heaven.

I normally go on retreats for about 3 days every quarter for prayers, meditation and rest. It's always a wonderful experience. I particularly enjoy the peace and tranquillity. There are no distractions. I am able to focus on God and myself. My time in retreat is usually filled with prayers, reading, meditation, relaxation and quietly sitting and watching nature around the centre. Sometimes I arrive at the retreat centre, tired and exhausted, by the time I leave, my body and energy is restored. My time at a retreat is always refreshing and peaceful. I always look forward to it. By the way I just realised I am due for the next retreat. Praise God! It's going to be a time of great refreshing from the Lord! I strongly recommend going on a retreat. Whether you are interested in time alone with God, relaxation or de-stressing, you will love it!

Your Miracle Moment

As I conclude this book, I perceive in my spirit that miracles are coming your way! Do you also perceive it? Expect and seize your miracle moments when they appear. I don't know what your situation, condition or problem is right now, but I know your miracles and desired solutions are closer than you may think, they are within your reach. Maybe you are thinking in your mind that your situation or problems need big faith to overcome. Well, not really.

The Bible records a statement by Jesus to His disciples in Matthew 17. This is what He says *"If you have faith as small as a mustard seed, you can say to this mountain, 'Move from here to there' and it will move; Nothing will be impossible for you."*

In His statement, Jesus was not referring to the acts of literally moving mountains, rather, He was speaking figuratively about the power of God when unleashed by faith. A 'Mountain' can figuratively represent a problem or a challenge or something that is overwhelming or seemingly impossible humanly speaking.

Have you seen a mustard seed? It is one of the smallest seeds in the world. It's only about 1 to 2 millimetres in diameter. As tiny as the seed is, it has the capacity to grow into a huge tree. It can produce trees that grow up to 20 feet tall and 20 feet wide. Just as the mustard seed with a tiny seed can produce a large tree, the smallest amount of faith placed in God who is able to make a tiny seed grow into a great tree can accomplish great things in your life! As far as God is concerned, it is not the size or quantity of your faith that will take Him to do the impossible in your life and situation, it is the quality of your faith. This means your confidence and trust in Him, His power and ability. It does not take big faith to produce great results; rather it takes a big and powerful God to produce great results. You don't need giant faith to receive from God, all you need is to call on Him for help and trust in His might and power to do wonders in your life and situation.

Do you feel like things are falling apart around you? Do you feel like your life is out of control? Do you feel like your situation is hopeless and your mountain seems insurmountable? Do not fear. Maybe all you need is a mustard seed faith, a seed of belief, a seed of trust in the all-powerful, all-knowing and all-sufficient God.

I believe you have that seed of faith in you right now. I am confident the truth and principles in this book are like mustard seeds that God can use to do mighty things in your life and situation. All you have to do is to exercise the faith and seize your miraculous moments when they present.

Think about the story of the woman with the issue of blood, healed miraculously by touching the cloth of Jesus. She sought medical solution to her problem. Despite previous disappointments from unsuccessful medical treatments and financial strains due to medical bills, she said to herself before touching the cloth of Jesus "If I can touch his clothes, I will, be healed". This was her mustard seed faith that produced the miracle healing that she desperately needed. She expected to be healed, she expected her turnaround. She expected a solution to her problem. She did not allow her past experience of financial losses, failures, mistakes and inadequacies of medical experts to rob her miracle. She did not allow opinion of others to rob her of her miraculous moment. She exercised her mustard seed faith, her mountain moved. Her story changed!

There is no situation so hopeless in your life that God cannot turnaround. There is nothing too hard or difficult for him. It does not matter how long you may have been waiting, I believe you are stepping into your God appointed moment of miracles and blessings. Let go of the past. Exercise the mustard seed faith in you! Reach out to God like the woman who had the issue of blood and you will experience the miraculous working power of God.

The Miracle of Life

Have you ever thought about the miracle of life? Your birth, your entrance into this world was a miracle. It marked the beginning of a unique opportunity for greatness and significance. Make this precious miracle of life count, don't let it slip away.

As Winston Churchill, former British Prime minister said "There comes a special moment in everyone's life, a moment for which that person was born. The special opportunity when he seized it fulfils his mission - a mission for which he is uniquely qualified. In that moment, he finds greatness. It is his finest hour."

Friend, this is your finest hour to fulfil your mission that you have been uniquely called and qualified by God. This is your moment to fulfil your destiny. Seize this moment!

You are born to reign
You are destined for greatness
You are destined for significance.

REFERENCES

Chapter One
1. https://en.wikipedia.org/wiki/Melanie_Amaro
2. Don Moen, God will make a way(2003)
3. http://top40.about.com/od/l/p/leonalewis.htm
4. Coming to America(Film) Eddie Murphy (1988)

Chapter Two
1. Venus Williams, Come to Win (2010)
2. Beyonce Knowles(quote)
3. https://en.wikipedia.org/wiki/Walt_Disney
4. https://en.wikipedia.org/wiki/Benson_Idahosa
5. Joel Osteen, Your Best Life Now(2004)
6. http://www.inc.com/business-insider/21-successful-people-who -rebounded-after-getting-fired.html
7. http://www.planetmotivation.com/never-quit.html
8. https://en.wikipedia.org/wiki/Sidney_Poitier

Chapter Three
1. Viktor Emil Frankl, Man's Search for Meaning
2. http://www.examiner.com/article/is-blaming-others-for-the-consequences-of-your-choices-kind-of-lame. (Article by Nicolas Roquefort- Villeneuve, relationship counsellor)
3. Stephen Covey, The 8th Habit: From Effectiveness to Greatness

Chapter Four
1. https://en.wikipedia.org/wiki/Andy_Murray
2. https://en.wikipedia.org/wiki/Muhammad_Ali

3. http://moneyweek.com/alexander-amosu-i-made-6-first-day-and-grew-from-there-44168/

4. http://www.alexanderamosu.co.uk/en/main.html#/home/

5. https://en.wikipedia.org/wiki/Colonel_Sanders

6. https://en.wikipedia.org/wiki/Nola_Ochs

7. https://en.wikipedia.org/wiki/Grandma_Moses

8. My life History, Paintings by Grandma Moses

9. https://en.wikipedia.org/wiki/Oscar_Pistorius

10. https://en.wikipedia.org/wiki/Nick_Vujicic

11. http://www.britannica.com/biography/T-M-Aluko

12. Colin Powell(Author of My American Journey)

13. http://www.managetrainlearn.com/article/put-gold-in-your-bank/

14. https://en.wikipedia.org/wiki/Henry_Ford

15. https://en.wikipedia.org/wiki/Florence_Nightingale

16. https://en.wikipedia.org/wiki/Michael_Johnson_(sprinter)

17. https://en.wikipedia.org/wiki/Kobe_Bryant

18. Kobe Bryant- The Interview with Ahmad Rashad

19. Daniel Coyle, The Little Book of Talent

20. John Maxwell, Beyond Talent.

Chapter Five

1. https://en.wikipedia.org/wiki/Martin_Luther_King,_J

2. https://en.wikipedia.org/wiki/I_Have_a_Dream

3. https://en.wikipedia.org/wiki/Henry_Ford

4. http://www.statesymbolsusa.org/symbol-official-item/ohio/state-motto-state-quarter/god-all-things-are-possible

5. https://en.wikipedia.org/wiki/Rosa_Parks

6. https://en.wikipedia.org/wiki/Mother_Teresa

7. https://en.wikipedia.org/wiki/Florence_Nightingale

Chapter Seven

1. Kris Vallatton, The Supernatural Power Of Forgiveness
2. Charles Dickens, Great Expectations
3. https://internationalforgiveness.wordpress.com/2013/09/22/enrights-forgiveness-intervention-the-results-were-glowing/
4. http://gimundo.com/news/article/hospice-nurse-reunites-with-long-lost-father-in-hospital-where-she-works/

Chapter Eight

1. https://en.wikipedia.org/wiki/J._K._Rowling
2. http://news.harvard.edu/gazette/story/2008/06/text-of-j-k-rowling-speech/
3. http://www.giantsforgod.com/peter-j-daniels/
4. https://en.wikipedia.org/wiki/Peter_J._Daniels
5. http://www.motivationalmemo.com/from-illiterate-bricklayer-to-international-business-statesman/
6. Mark Victor Hanson & Robert G Allen, Cracking the Millionaire Code(2005)
7. Watty Piper, The Little Engine That Could.

Chapter Nine

1. Edgar Albert Guest , Don't Quit , 1921 (Poem)
2. https://en.wikipedia.org/wiki/Sylvester_Stallone
3. http://www.endlesshumanpotential.com/sylvester-stallone-story.html
4. https://en.wikipedia.org/wiki/Stevie_Wonder
5. http://www.history-of-rock.com/stevie_wondertwo.htm
6. https://en.wikipedia.org/wiki/Nelson_Mandela
7. https://en.wikipedia.org/wiki/Edmund_Hillary
8. http://zchris2015.weebly.com/sir-edmund-hillary.html
9. Og Mandino, Greatest Salesman In the World

Chapter Ten

1. Richard Mahler, Stillness: Daily Gifts of Solitude
2. www.jkrowling.com

THANK YOU

I hope you enjoyed reading this book and found it inspiring. If you have any comments, feedback or enquiries, please feel free to contact me via email: joseph.agunbiade2015@gmail.com.

To order products, or for any other correspondence, please contact candopublishers@gmail.com.

CPSIA information can be obtained
at www.ICGtesting.com
Printed in the USA
LVOW07s1732170817
545388LV00012B/888/P